General Knowledge Olympiad

Class 05

A must have book for all
Olympiads & Talent Search Exams...

by
Nandini Sharma

BLoOM CAP
Bloom Cap Edu Ventures Pvt. Ltd.

Bloom Cap Edu Ventures Pvt. Ltd.

卐 **Administrative & Production Office**

'Ramchhaya' 4577/15, Agarwal Road, Darya Ganj, New Delhi -110002
Tele: 011- 47630600, 43518550

卐 **ISBN :** 978-93-25519-44-2

卐 **PRICE :** ₹100.00

卐 **PO No :** TXT-XX-XXXXXXX-X-XX

For further information about the books log on to
www.bloomcap.org

Follow us on   

Preface

"Future belongs to those Who prepares for it today"

School Olympiads are National & International level competitions conducted by different Government, Non-Government & Educational Organisations with the purpose of making the children ready to face competitive exams. The challenging Questions asked in Olympiads motivate them to learn more & more and bring out the best result with improved academic performance. The Awards & Scholarship offered by Olympiads motivate children to aspire & strive for doing better and emerge out to be the best.

GK Olympiads

GK is the knowledge of every aspect of the human life, which may or may not be the part of routine academic studies but very important for the overall personality development of the students. It is more or less connected with the attentiveness and awareness. There can be different domains of GK like; History, Geography, Polity, Culture, Discovery, Sports, Current Affairs etc.

GK Olympiads help students in understanding the importance of General Knowledge and updations about National & International Affairs in daily life..

'Bloom GK Olympiad Study Book Class 5' is a perfect resource to Study & Practice for Olympiad Exams and other National & State Level Talent Search Exams & Other Competitions.

Some Special Features of Bloom GK Olympiad Study Books are;

- Complete coverage of all the topics related to GK;. History, Geography, Environment, Polity, Science, Culture, Sports, etc.
- Chapterwise Exercises having different types of Objective Questions.
- Olympiad Pattern Practice Sets at the end.

This book is prepared by Expert Panel with the utmost care, still if you have any suggestions regarding its improvement then feel free to contact us at olympiads@bloomcap.org. We will try to inculcate your suggestions in the further editions.

Contents

01.	Famous Rulers and Freedom Fighters	1-3
02.	Religion and Culture	4-6
03.	Buildings & Monuments	7-10
04.	Solar System	11-13
05.	Earth and its Movement	14-15
06.	Continents and Oceans	16-17
07.	Rivers and Lakes	18-19
08.	Our Environment	20-22
09.	Our Government	23-24
10.	General Science	25-28
11.	Computers	29-31
12.	General Knowledge	32-36
13.	Books and Authors	37-38
14.	Important Days and Dates	39-41
15.	Awards and Honours	42-43
16.	Sports	44-46
•	**Practice Set 1**	**47-51**
•	**Practice Set 2**	**52-56**
•	**Answers**	**57-59**

Famous Rulers and Freedom Fighters

1 Mark Questions

1. Who was the founder of Mauryan Dynasty?
(a) Akbar
(b) Ashoka
(c) Chandragupta Maurya
(d) Porus

2. Sanchi Stupa in Madhya Pradesh was built by the Great Mauryan Emperor who is known as ....
(a) Ashoka   (b) Akbar
(c) Maharana Pratap (d) Shah Jahan

3. The first woman ruler of Delhi was...... .
(a) Mumtaz Mahal   (b) Noor Jahan
(c) Razia Sultana   (d) None of these

4. Who was the founder of Mughal Dynasty?
(a) Babur   (b) Humayun
(c) Akbar   (d) Jahangir

5. Who among the following was the son of Emperor Babur?
(a) Akbar   (b) Humayun
(c) Shah Jahan   (d) Aurangzeb

6. Choose the incorrect statement from the given options regarding Emperor Akbar.
(a) Birbal was one of the Navratna in Akbar's court.
(b) He built the Red Fort.
(c) Akbar was married to Jodhabai.
(d) He was the son of Humayun.

7. Structures like Taj Mahal, Jama Masjid, Red Fort were built by ....
(a) Jahangir   (b) Akbar
(c) Shah Jahan   (d) Humayun

8. Read the description below and identify the given personality.
He was a ruler of Rajasthan. His famous and loyal horse Chetak gave up his life to save him.
(a) Maharana Pratap
(b) Shivaji
(c) Bajirao
(d) Alauddin Khilji

9. Who was the founder of Maratha Empire?
(a) Bajirao
(b) Shivaji
(c) Ashoka
(d) Peshwa

10. Which Great King fought a war against Kalinga?
(a) Akbar
(b) Chandragupt Maurya
(c) Ashoka
(d) Shivaji

11. Identify the freedom fighter of 1857 revolt who was an Indian soldier in the British Army.

(a) Mangal Pandey (b) Bahadur Shah Zafar
(c) Kunwar Singh (d) Nana Sahib

12. A prominent female ruler whose real name was Manikarnika. She is ....
(a) Rani Lakshmibai
(b) Begum Hazrat Mahal
(c) Shobha Devi
(d) None of the above

13. Which of the following are remembered together?
(a) Shaheed Bhagat Singh, Sukhdev and Rajguru
(b) Chandra Shekhar Azad, Sukhdev and Mahatma Gandhi
(c) Mahatma Gandhi, Bhagat Singh and Jawaharlal Nehru
(d) Kunwar Singh, Tatyatope and Rajguru

14. Identify the freedom struggle leader of Indian National Congress in the given picture.

(a) Gopal Krishna Gokhale
(b) Jawaharlal Nehru
(c) Lala Lajpat Rai
(d) Mahatma Gandhi

15. Which among the following leaders started the Non-Cooperation Movement?
(a) Jawaharlal Nehru
(b) Bal Gangadhar Tilak
(c) Mahatma Gandhi
(d) Lala Lajpat Rai

16. Which Indian freedom fighter is known as "Shaheed-e-Azam"?
(a) Bhagat Singh
(b) Chandra Shekhar Azad
(c) Sardar Vallabhbhai Patel
(d) Mahatma Gandhi

17. Identify the leader who led the Azad Hind Fauj and fought for India's Freedom.
(a) Jawaharlal Nehru
(b) Netaji Subhash Chandra Bose
(c) Sardar Vallabhbhai Patel
(d) Mahatma Gandhi

18. Which freedom fighter said, "Dushman ki goliyon ka hum samna karenge, Azad hee rahein hain, Azad hee rahenge"?
(a) Jawaharlal Nehru
(b) Bhagat Singh
(c) Bipin Chandra Pal
(d) Chandra Shekhar Azad

19. Who among the following freedom fighter was also called 'Punjab Kesari' and 'Lion of Punjab'?
(a) Mahatma Gandhi
(b) Lala Lajpat Rai
(c) Vallabhbhai Patel
(d) Jawaharlal Nehru

20. Which of the following statements is incorrect about Mahatma Gandhi?
(a) He is known as Father of the Nation.
(b) He worked on the principles of violence.
(c) He led several movements for a free India.
(d) He was a lawyer by profession.

21. Which freedom fighter is also known as the Nightingale of India or Bharat Kokila?
    (a) Sarojini Naidu
    (b) Annie Besant
    (c) Kasturba Gandhi
    (d) Kamla Nehru

22. He was the first nationalist freedom fighter who brought the concept of 'Swaraj'. He is ....

    (a) Bal Gangadhar Tilak
    (b) Subhash Chandra Bose
    (c) Jawaharlal Nehru
    (d) Bipin Chandra Pal

23. Which of the following freedom movement leaders is also known as the Iron Man of India?
    (a) Jawaharlal Nehru
    (b) Sardar Vallabhbhai Patel
    (c) Mahatma Gandhi
    (d) Subhash Chandra Bose

2 Marks Questions

24. Read the description and identify the personality.

    He was the second Prime Minister of India. He gave the slogan 'Jai Jawan Jai Kisan'. He was a freedom fighter.
    (a) Bhagat Singh
    (b) Morarji Desai
    (c) Lal Bahadur Shastri
    (d) Sarvepalli Radhakrishnan

25. Read the description and identify the fighter. He is known for raising his voice against the injustice caused to untouchables. He was a lawyer and was popularly known as BabaSaheb.
    (a) Jawaharlal Nehru
    (b) Mahatma Gandhi
    (c) BR Ambedkar   (d) GK Gokhale

26. Which of the following pairs is incorrectly matched?

    (a) Bhagat Singh   – Shaheed-e-Azam

    (b) Bipin Chandra Pal   – Pal in (Lal-Bal-Pal)

    (c) Gopal Krishna   – Gold of India
        Gokhale

    (d) Subhas Chandra Bose – Netaji

27. Identify the leaders 'X' and 'Y'.
    'X' gave the slogan 'Inquilab Zindabad' and 'Y' gave the slogan 'Araam Haraam Hai'.

    (a) Chandra Shekhar Azad and Jawaharlal Nehru
    (b) Bhagat Singh and Jawaharlal Nehru
    (c) Chandra Shekhar Azad and Motilal Nehru
    (d) Bhagat Singh and Mahatma Gandhi

28. Match the following.

List I (Freedom Fighters)		List II (Slogans)
A.	Bhagat Singh	1. "Tum Mujhe Khoon Do, Main Tumhe Azadi Doonga". (Give me blood and I will give you freedom)
B.	Netaji Subhash Chandra Bose	2. Inquilab Zindabad
C.	Mahatma Gandhi	3. Swaraj Mera Janamsiddh Adhikar Hai, Aur Main Ise Lekar Rahunga
D.	Bal Gangadhar Tilak	4. 'Do or die' (Karo Ya Maro)

Codes

	A	B	C	D
(a)	1	2	3	4
(b)	2	1	4	3
(c)	4	1	2	3
(d)	3	4	1	2

Religion and Culture

1 Mark Questions

1. Which of the following Vedas was compiled first?
   (a) Rigveda   (b) Samaveda
   (c) Yajurveda   (d) Atharvaveda

2. The Vedic deity Indra is known as the God of.............. .
   (a) wind
   (b) fire
   (c) rain and thunder
   (d) energy

3. In Hindu mythology, who is the God of death?
   (a) Indra   (b) Saraswati
   (c) Yama   (d) Brahma

4. Who is the Goddess of speech, wisdom and learning?
   (a) Shasti   (b) Saraswati
   (c) Satyanarayana   (d) Savitar

5. The 'Three Jewels' (Triratnas) of Jainism are.............. .
   (a) Right Action, Right Livelihood and Right Effort
   (b) Right Speech, Right Thinking and Right Behaviour
   (c) Right Faith, Right Knowledge and Right Conduct
   (d) None of the above

6. Identify the tree where Gautama Buddha gained knowledge and became enlightened.

   (a) Bodhi tree   (b) Neem tree
   (c) Holy basil   (d) Peepal tree

7. Which one of the following is not included in the Eight Fold Path of Buddhism?
   (a) Right Speech   (b) Right Desire
   (c) Right Conduct   (d) Right View

8. Read the description and identify the personality.

   The famous Bhakti Saint who was a great devotee of Lord Krishna. She belonged to the royal family of Mewar, she is ....
   (a) Ramabai   (b) Mirabai
   (c) Radhabai   (d) None of these

9. Read the description and identify the personality.

   He preached Bhakti/ Devotion through the medium of his Dohas. He is ....
   (a) Kabir Das
   (b) Bhagat Namdev
   (c) Ramananda
   (d) Sri Ramanuja

10. Read the description and identify the Sikh Guru.

    He was the founder of Sikh religion and the first Guru of Sikhism. He is ....
    (a) Guru Nanak
    (b) Guru Gobind Singh
    (c) Guru Teg Bahadur
    (d) Guru Hargobind

11. Who among the following was the tenth Guru of Sikh religion?
    (a) Guru Teg Bahadur
    (b) Guru Nanak
    (c) Guru Gobind Singh
    (d) Guru Hargobind

12. The largest Buddhist Monastery in India is located at
    (a) Gangtok, Sikkim
    (b) Dharamshala, Himachal Pradesh
    (c) Tawang, Arunachal Pradesh
    (d) Sarnath, Uttar Pradesh

13. The famous play dance Raslila belongs to which state?
    (a) Haryana   (b) Uttar Pradesh
    (c) Gujarat   (d) Tamil Nadu

14. Classical dance 'Mohiniyattam' belongs to which state?
    (a) Kerala   (b) Andhra Pradesh
    (c) Manipur   (d) Punjab

15. Which classical dance form is famous in Uttar Pradesh?
    (a) Kathak
    (b) Kuchipudi
    (c) Bhangra
    (d) Garba

16. Which of the following combinations of the states and the festivals mainly celebrated there, is not correct?
    (a) Assam – Bihu
    (b) Maharashtra – Ganesh Chaturthi
    (c) Gujarat – Durga Puja
    (d) Rajasthan – Gangaur

17. The Ram Utsav, a famous fair is held in which state every year?
    (a) Odisha
    (b) Gujarat
    (c) Manipur
    (d) Assam

18. Which among the following annual fairs of Rajasthan is famous for its camel trading event?
    (a) Pushkar Mela
    (b) Kumbha Mela
    (c) Surajkund Mela
    (d) Ganga Sagar Mela

19. Which among the following places represent the contemporary four Dhams of Hindu Pilgrimage in India?
    (a) Amarnath, Kedarnath, Vaishno-devi and Gangotri
    (b) Badrinath, Kedarnath, Gangotri and Yamunotri
    (c) Kashi Vishwanath, Jagganath Puri, Rameshwaram and Akshardham
    (d) Shirdi, Tirupati-Balaji, Somnath and Amarnath

20. Which form of dance is depicted in the picture shown below?

(a) Kathakali
(b) Kuchipudi
(c) Kathak
(d) Bharatanatyam

21. In which of the following festivals, boat races are a special feature?
(a) Pongal
(b) Onam
(c) Bihu
(d) Holi

22. The Rath Yatra at Puri is celebrated in honour of which Hindu deity?
(a) Ram
(b) Jagganath
(c) Shiva
(d) Vishnu

23. The last day of Durga Puja is known as ....
(a) Navami
(b) Panchmi
(c) Ashtmi
(d) Dashmi

24. Which among the following is the popular dance form of Maharashtra's musical theatre?
(a) Gatha
(b) Tamasha
(c) Nautanki
(d) Lavani

25. Which is the most ancient musical instrument of India?
(a) Veena (b) Flute (c) Sitar (d) Tabla

26. In which state is the folk painting 'Madhubani' popular?
(a) Assam
(b) Bihar
(c) West Bengal
(d) Odisha

2 Marks Questions

27. Which of the following pairs is correctly matched?
(a) Mizoram – Gudi Padwa
(b) Nagaland – Hornbill Festival
(c) Tripura – Onam
(d) Assam – Braj Festival

28. In which of the following styles of dance, the theme is always taken from Mahabharata and Ramayana?
(a) Mohiniyattam
(b) Bharatanatyam
(c) Kathakali
(d) Kuchipudi

29. Identify the state to which this traditional dress 'Puan' given in the image belongs.

(a) Tripura
(b) Meghalaya
(c) Mizoram
(d) Assam

30. Which of the following places of Sikh religious heritage is not in India?
(a) Nankana Sahib
(b) Shishganj Sahib
(c) Bangla Sahib
(d) Sri Harminder Sahib (Golden Temple)

Chapter 03

Buildings and Monuments

1 Mark Questions

1. Which among the following is one of the tallest brick and stone minarets in the world located in New Delhi?
   (a) Taj Mahal   (b) Qutub Minar
   (c) Jama Masjid   (d) Humayun's Tomb

2. The 'Statue of Unity' known as the tallest statue in the world is located in
   ....
   (a) Gujarat   (b) Rajasthan
   (c) Bihar   (d) New Delhi

3. It is also known as 'Tower of Fame'. Identify the monument.
   (a) Qutub Minar   (b) Vijaya Stambh
   (c) Deep Stambh   (d) Rajput Stambh

4. Jantar Mantar, located in New Delhi, Ujjain, Mathura and Jaipur is ....
   (a) an astronomical observatory
   (b) a museum
   (c) a fort
   (d) a mughal Garden

5. One of the most ancient and celebrated religious buildings of Goa. This is ...... largest church in Goa.
   (a) Se Cathedral
   (b) St. Paul's Cathedral
   (c) Santa Cruz Basilica
   (d) Basilica of Bom Jesus

6. Which of the following is the oldest stone structure in India?
   (a) Taj Mahal   (b) Qutub Minar
   (c) Red Fort   (d) Sanchi Stupa

7. Which building is known as 'White Marble Mughal Architecture'?
   (a) Taj Mahal   (b) Qutub Minar
   (c) Charminar Fort   (d) Ajanta

8. Which heritage site is well known for its stepped corridors, sculptures and stone carvings in the well?
   (a) Buland Darwaza (b) Rani Ki Vav
   (c) Fatehpur Sikri   (d) Sun Temple

9. Which of the following is India's largest and oldest Museum?
   (a) Indian Museum, Kolkata
   (b) National Museum, New Delhi
   (c) National Rail Museum, New Delhi
   (d) Assam State Museum, Guwahati

10. Read the description and identify the monument.
    It is also referred as 'The Taj Mahal of Mumbai'. It is ....
    (a) Gateway of India
    (b) Elephanta Caves
    (c) Bandra Fort
    (d) None of the above

11. It is the tallest free-standing structure in the world with 160 floors. It is ....
(a) Empire State Building, New York
(b) Shanghai Tower, China
(c) Burj Khalifa, United Arab Emirates
(d) Eiffel Tower, France

12. Read the description and identify the memorial.
It is the venue for hoisting the Indian Flag on Independence Day parade. It is ....
(a) Red Fort
(b) Victoria Memorial
(c) Gateway of India
(d) Vivekananda Rock Memorial

13. It is famous as the ancient seat of learning situated in Bihar. This is known as ....
(a) Taxila   (b) Nalanda
(c) Vikramshila   (d) Vallabhi

14. It is the highest entrance gate of its kind in the entire world. This monument is ....
(a) Agra Fort
(b) Buland Darwaza
(c) Humayun's Tomb
(d) Jama Masjid

15. Which of the following monument is located in Fatehpur Sikri?
(a) Red Fort
(b) Humayun's Tomb
(c) Bibi ka Maqbara
(d) Buland Darwaza

16. This Fort is known as 'Great Wall of India' located in Rajasthan. It is ....
(a) Jaisalmer Fort
(b) Kumbhalgarh Fort
(c) Humayun's Tomb
(d) Fatehpur Sikri

17. Which of the following is the 'First Garden Tomb' built in India?
(a) Humayun's Tomb
(b) Bibi ka Maqbara
(c) Purana Qila
(d) Akbar's Tomb

18. Identify the Fort which is located in Uttar Pradesh and was built by the Mughals.

(a) Jhansi Fort   (b) Agra Fort
(c) Red Fort   (d) Gwalior Fort

19. The 'Largest Fort' in India and a World Heritage site is ....
(a) Red Fort
(b) Gwalior Fort
(c) Chittorgarh Fort
(d) Jhansi Fort

20. Identify the monument from the description and image given below.
It is the largest amphitheatre in the world, it is ....

(a) Amphitheatre of Pompeii
(b) Colosseum
(c) The Globe
(d) None of the above

21. This monument is also known as the 'Diamond of Kollur Mine'. It is located in Hyderabad. It is ....
    (a) Golconda Fort   (b) Kumbalgarh Fort
    (c) Jaisalmer Fort   (d) Agra Fort

22. Which of the following places was carlier known as Victoria Terminus?
    (a) Chhatrapati Shivaji Terminus
    (b) Gateway of India
    (c) Soneri Mahal
    (d) Town Hall

23. It is one of the 'Oldest Churches' in India. It is also a World Heritage site located in Goa. This is ....
    (a) Santa Cruz Basilica
    (b) Basilica of Bom Jesus
    (c) St. Francis Church
    (d) St. Paul Cathedral

24. It is also called the 'Tomb of the Lady' located in Aurangabad, Maharashtra. This is ....
    (a) Bibi ka Maqbara (b) Akbar's Tomb
    (c) Humayun's Tomb (d) Taj Mahal

25. Read the description and identify the building given in the picture.

    It is a place of worship and meditation for every religion. It is ....

    (a) Lotus Temple
    (b) Sun Temple
    (c) Suraj Kund
    (d) None of these

26. It is one of the most 'Haunted Fort' in India located in Rajasthan. It is ....
    (a) Kumbalgarh Fort
    (b) Jaisalmer Fort
    (c) Bhangarh Fort
    (d) Mehrangarh Fort

2 Marks Questions

27. It is one of the most magnificent structures in Lucknow. It is also known as Bhool Bhulaiya with 1024 ways of going in and only 2 to come out. It is ....
    (a) Bara Imambara
    (b) Moti Masjid
    (c) Chota Imambara
    (d) Sheesh Mahal

28. The temple shown in the image is located in which state?

    (a) Orissa   (b) Jharkhand
    (c) Gujarat   (d) Karnataka

29. Find the incorrect matching pair.
    (a) Agrasen ki Baoli – Madhya Pradesh
    (b) Bibi ka Maqbara – Maharashtra
    (c) Char Minar   – Telangana
    (d) Dilwara Jain   – Rajasthan
        Temple

30. 'X' and 'Y' caves are located in Maharashtra. These caves comprises of Buddhist, Jain and Hindu cave temples. Identify 'X' and 'Y'.
    (a) Ajanta and Ellora
    (b) Elephanta and Ajanta
    (c) Ellora and Elephanta
    (d) Ajanta and Amarnath

31. Match the following.

List I (Modern Architecture)		List II (Location)
A. Humayun's Tomb	1.	Agra
B. Fatehpur Sikri	2.	Hyderabad
C. Mecca Masjid	3.	Madhya Pradesh
D. Sanchi Stupa	4.	New Delhi

Codes

	A	B	C	D
(a)	2	3	4	1
(b)	3	4	1	2
(c)	1	2	3	4
(d)	4	1	2	3

Solar System

1 Mark Questions

1. The path along which planet revolve around the Sun is known as ....
   (a) axis
   (b) orbit
   (c) circle
   (d) None of these

2. Which of these is the Natural Satellite of Earth?
   (a) Stars
   (b) Sun
   (c) Moon
   (d) INSAT

3. Which of these planet is not made up of gases?
   (a) Jupiter
   (b) Uranus
   (c) Neptune
   (d) Mars

4. I revolve around the Sun. I am the first number of the Solar System. Who am I?
   (a) Mars
   (b) Mercury
   (c) Jupiter
   (d) None of these

5. Which of the following is not a Jovian planet?
   (a) Venus
   (b) Uranus
   (c) Saturn
   (d) Jupiter

6. The planets on either side of the Earth are ....
   (a) Mercury and Venus
   (b) Mars and Jupiter
   (c) Mars and Venus
   (d) Venus and Saturn

7. Which of the following planets have no Moons?
   (a) Mars and Jupiter
   (b) Mercury and Venus
   (c) Pluto and Mars
   (d) Mars and Venus

8. Read the description and identify the image given below.
   It is also popular as "Shooting Stars" and normally seen in the upper atmosphere. It is ....
   (a) Comets
   (b) Meteors
   (c) Asteroids
   (d) Orbit

9. Which of the following is the smallest planet in our Solar System?
   (a) Mercury
   (b) Venus
   (c) Neptune
   (d) Uranus

10. It is a group of stars that forms a pattern. This is known as ....
    (a) Galaxy
    (b) Constellations
    (c) Satellite
    (d) Asteroids

11. Which planet was redefined as a 'Dwarf planet'?
    (a) Neptune   (b) Uranus
    (c) Pluto   (d) Saturn

12. Which of the following does not have its own light?
    (a) Moon   (b) Star
    (c) Sun   (d) None of these

13. Which of the following are also known as small planets or planetoids largely found in between Mars and Jupiter?
    (a) Comets
    (b) Meteors
    (c) Asteroids
    (d) None of the above

14. Which of the following heavenly body is made up of millions of stars?
    (a) Sun   (b) Black Hole
    (c) Galaxy   (d) Solar System

15. Which of the following planets has a lesser rotation time than the Earth?
    (a) Jupiter   (b) Mars
    (c) Mercury   (d) Venus

16. Identify the Constellation given in the image below.

    (a) Orion   (b) Ursa Major
    (c) Ursa Minor   (d) None of these

17. Which planet rotates in an opposite direction to that of Earth?
    (a) Mercury   (b) Venus
    (c) Jupiter   (d) Neptune

18. Lunar Eclipse can be seen when there is ....
    (a) half moon
    (b) full moon
    (c) new moon
    (d) crescent moon

19. Solar Eclipse occurs when ....
    (a) Moon comes in between Earth and Sun.
    (b) Earth comes in between Moon and Sun.
    (c) Sun comes in between Earth and Moon.
    (d) Sun rays do not reach Earth.

20. Consider the following statements and choose the correct option.
    (a) Stars are celestial bodies that continuously emit light and heat.
    (b) Sun is the only star in the Solar System.
    (c) Stars are not visible from naked eyes.
    (d) None of the above

21. We can see full Moon in every ....
    (a) 12 days   (b) 15 days
    (c) 29.5 days   (d) 16 days

22. Which planet is known as sleeping planet?
    (a) Mars
    (b) Neptune
    (c) Earth
    (d) Mercury

23. The different forms of Moon are shown in the image, identify the Crescent Moon.

(a)

(b)

(c)

(d) None of the above

24. Choose the correct order of planets from the Sun.
(a) Mercury, Venus, Earth, Mars, Jupiter
(b) Venus, Mercury, Earth, Mars, Jupiter
(c) Mercury, Venus, Mars, Earth, Jupiter
(d) Venus, Mercury, Mars, Jupiter, Earth

2 Marks Questions

25. Find the correct pair.
1. Asteroids–Revolves around Neptune
2. Moon–Revolves around Earth
3. Mars–Revolves around Sun
Codes
(a) Only 1 and 2
(b) Only 2 and 3
(c) Only 1 and 3
(d) All of the above

26. The surface of the Moon is covered with which of the following?
(a) Water   (b) Soil
(c) Craters   (d) All of these

27. Which of the given statements is correct?
1. The outermost layer of Sun is called Corona.
2. The Sun is the only star in Milky Way Galaxy.

Codes
(a) Only 1
(b) Only 2
(c) Both 1 and 2
(d) None of the above

28. Consider the following statements.
1. Jupiter is the largest planet in the Solar System.
2. Mercury is the hottest planet in the Solar System.
3. Saturn is popular for its spectacular ring system.
4. Mars is known as 'Blue Planet'.
Which of the statements given above is/are correct?
(a) Both 1 and 3   (b) Only 2
(c) Only 4   (d) None of these

29. Match the following.

List I	List II
A. Saturn	1. Largest planet
B. Jupiter	2. Last planet
C. Neptune	3. Nearest planet to Sun
D. Mercury	4. Second largest planet

Codes

	A	B	C	D		A	B	C	D
(a)	4	1	2	3	(b)	1	2	3	4
(c)	3	1	2	4	(d)	4	3	2	1

Chapter 05

Earth and its Movement

1 Mark Questions

1. What is the shape of the Earth?
   (a) Sphere   (b) Ellipsoid
   (c) Circular   (d) Spiral

2. Movement of the Earth on its axis is called as ....
   (a) Revolution   (b) Equinox
   (c) Rotation   (d) Great Circle

3. The Earth rotates in which direction on its axis?
   (a) North to South (b) West to East
   (c) East to West   (d) South to North

4. The shape of Earth's Orbit is ....
   (a) circular   (b) elliptical
   (c) rectangular   (d) semi-circular

5. .... is an imaginary line which divides the Earth into Eastern and Western hemisphere.
   (a) Equator   (b) Prime Meridian
   (c) Tropic of Cancer (d) Latitude

6. .... Eclipse occurs when the Earth comes in between the Sun and the Moon.
   (a) Solar   (b) Lunar
   (c) Earth   (d) None of these

7. Which of the following helps to calculate time of a place?
   (a) Longitudes   (b) Latitudes
   (c) Both (a) and (b) (d) None of these

8. This Meridian is called International Date Line. It is ....
   (a) 90°   (b) 180°
   (c) 360°   (d) None of these

9. Which among the following meet at the Poles?
   (a) Equator
   (b) Longitudes
   (c) Latitudes
   (d) None of the above

10. The movement of the Earth around the Sun is known as ....
    (a) Revolution   (b) Rotation
    (c) Axis   (d) Orbit

11. Leap year is repeated after how many years?
    (a) Two years   (b) Three years
    (c) Four years   (d) Five years

12. The period between day and night is called ....
    (a) Axis   (b) Orbit (c) Dusk (d) Dawn

13. The plane formed by the axis of Earth and Orbit is known as the ....
    (a) Orbital plane
    (b) Spherical plane
    (c) Symmetric plane
    (d) None of the above

14. Choose the incorrect statement from the given options.
(a) Seasons are caused due to rotation of the Earth.
(b) Rotation causes day and night.
(c) The Earth rotates on its axis.
(d) Rotation also influences the flow of ocean currents.

15. The word equinox means equal ....
(a) days
(b) months
(c) day and night
(d) None of these

16. On 21st March, we have .... equinox.
(a) Autumnal
(b) Summer
(c) Spring
(d) Winter

17. The Prime Meridian is also known as ....
(a) Latin Meridian
(b) Greenwich Meridian
(c) Arctic Meridian
(d) Antarctic Meridian

18. Which movement of Earth is responsible for light and darkness?
(a) Revolution
(b) Rotation
(c) Tectonic Movement
(d) None of these

19. The Earth's axis is an invisible line that intersects the Earth throughout both X and Y poles. Identify X and Y.
(a) East, West
(b) East, North
(c) North, South
(d) South, West

20. How many days does the Moon require to complete one revolution around the Earth?
(a) 27   (b) 64   (c) 31   (d) 30

21. The revolution of the Earth gives us which season/s?
(a) Summer
(b) Winter
(c) Autumn
(d) All of the above

2 Marks Questions

22. Match the following.

	List I		List II
A.	Earth revolves from	1.	Elliptical
B.	Earth's orbit is	2.	Keeps on changing
C.	Distance between Earth and Sun	3.	West to East

Codes

	A	B	C
(a)	1	2	3
(b)	3	1	2
(c)	3	2	1
(d)	2	3	1

23. Which of the following best describes an Earthquake?
(a) An opening in the Earth's crust where Magma erupts to the surface.
(b) A violent shaking of the Earth when two tectonic plates bump into each other.
(c) A large storm with very high speed winds.
(d) A downward movement of rock, debris and soil. +

24. Which of the following is true for rotation of Earth?
(a) Spinning of Earth around its axis
(b) Spinning of Earth around Sun
(c) Spinning of Earth around stars
(d) Spinning of Earth around Galaxy

Chapter 06

Continents and Oceans

1 Mark Questions

1. Which continent has the largest number of population living in it?
   (a) Africa   (c) North America
   (c) Asia   (d) Europe

2. The Smallest Continent in the world is ....
   (a) Europe   (b) Australia
   (c) Antarctica   (d) Asia

3. The continent of North America is separated from South America by ....
   (a) Suez Canel
   (b) Panama Canal
   (c) Stockholm Canal
   (d) Nan Madol Canal

4. The only continent in the world without a desert is ....
   (a) Europe   (b) Africa
   (c) Asia   (d) Australia

5. The famous Amazon rainforests are found in this continent. It is ....
   (a) Antarctica   (b) South America
   (c) North America   (d) Australia

6. Which continent is also known as the 'Continent of Thirsty Lands'?
   (a) Asia   (b) Australia
   (c) North America   (d) Europe

7. The Coldest Continent on the Earth is ....
   (a) Europe   (b) South America
   (c) North America   (d) Antarctica

8. Which continents are completely North of the Equator?
   (a) North America, Europe, and Asia
   (b) South America, Asia and Africa
   (c) Australia, Africa and Antarctica
   (d) None of the above

9. Which continents are completely South of the Equator?
   (a) Asia and Europe
   (b) Australia and Antarctica
   (c) North America and South America
   (d) Africa and Europe

10. Which continent is also known as 'Bird Continent'?
    (a) Europe   (b) Asia
    (c) Africa   (d) South America

11. The continent through which both the Tropic of Cancer and Tropic of Capricorn passes is ....
    (a) North America
    (b) Asia
    (c) Africa
    (d) Australia

12. In which of the following continents river Nile and Sahara Desert are found?
    (a) Asia   (b) Australia
    (c) Europe   (d) Africa

13. The deepest point on Earth, 'Mariana Trench' is located in which ocean?
    (a) Arctic   (b) Indian
    (c) Pacific   (d) Atlantic

14. World's largest desert 'Sahara' is found in this continent. It is ....
    (a) Europe   (b) Australia
    (c) Asia   (d) Africa

15. Mount Everest is located in which continent?
    (a) Africa   (b) Asia
    (c) Europe   (d) Antarctica

16. The two important parts of this ocean are the Arabian Sea and Bay of Bengal. This is ....
    (a) Pacific ocean   (b) Arctic ocean
    (c) Indian ocean   (d) Atlantic ocean

17. This ocean is shaped like the letter 'S'. It is ....
    (a) Arctic ocean   (b) Atlantic ocean
    (c) Pacific ocean   (d) Indian ocean

18. Which of the following is the smallest ocean of the world?
    (a) Pacific ocean   (b) Indian ocean
    (c) Atlantic ocean (d) Arctic ocean

19. What is the name of the warm ocean current that flows across the Atlantic?
    (a) Gulf stream
    (b) Labrador current
    (c) Kuroshio current
    (d) California current

20. Which of the ocean is named after a country?
    (a) Arctic Ocean   (b) Southern Ocean
    (c) Indian Ocean   (d) Pacific Ocean

21. Which ocean is frozen for most part of the year?
    (a) Pacific ocean   (b) Atlantic ocean
    (c) Indian ocean   (d) Arctic ocean

2 Marks Questions

22. Consider the following statements.
    1. There are only 3 oceans in the world.
    2. Arctic ocean is the smallest ocean.
    3. Pacific ocean covers the largest area of the planet's surface.

    Which of the following statements is/are correct?
    (a) Only 1   (b) Only 2
    (c) Both 2 and 3   (d) Neither 1 nor 2

23. Find the pair which matched correctly?
    | Continent | Mountain |
    (a) Asia   – K2
    (b) North America – Mount Albert
    (c) South America – Cotopaxi
    (d) All of the above

24. Match the following correctly

List I (Ocean)	List II (Feature)
A. Pacific Ocean	1. Deepest Ocean
B. Atlantic Ocean	2. Coldest Ocean
C. Arctic Ocean	3. Second largest Ocean

Codes

	A	B	C			A	B	C
(a)	1	2	3		(b)	3	2	1
(c)	1	3	2		(d)	2	3	1

Rivers and Lakes

1 Mark Questions

1. Which among the following rivers is the 'National River of India'?
   (a) Yamuna   (b) Narmada
   (c) Ganga   (d) Brahmaputra

2. Delhi is located on the bank of which river?
   (a) Kaveri   (b) Krishna
   (c) Yamuna   (d) Brahmaputra

3. How many rivers meet at Triveni or Sangam?
   (a) 7   (b) 8   (c) 3   (d) 4

4. The largest tributary of Ganga is ....
   (a) Yamuna   (b) Narmada
   (c) Brahmaputra   (d) Saraswati

5. The Bhakra Nangal Dam is the second highest dam which is built on .... river.
   (a) Ganga   (b) Yamuna
   (c) Brahmaputra   (d) Sutlej

6. In which state Bhagirathi and Alaknanda rivers combine to form Ganga river?
   (a) Assam
   (b) Uttarakhand
   (c) Jammu and Kashmir
   (d) Arunachal Pradesh

7. On which river 'Howrah Bridge' is situated?
   (a) Yamuna   (b) Hooghly
   (c) Brahmaputra   (d) Sutlej

8. India's highest waterfall 'Jog Falls' is located in ....
   (a) Maharashtra
   (b) Madhya Pradesh
   (c) Karnataka
   (d) Himachal Pradesh

9. Which river is also known as Dakshin Ganga?
   (a) Krishna   (b) Kaveri
   (c) Godavari   (d) Mahanadi

10. The Sutlej river is sometimes known as the ....
    (a) Blue river   (b) White river
    (c) Green river   (d) Red river

11. Which of the following is the largest fresh water lake of Asia?
    (a) Pushkar lake   (b) Chilka lake
    (c) Wular lake   (d) Pangong lake

12. Where is the 'Dul lake' situated in India?
    (a) Gujarat
    (b) Jammu and Kashmir
    (c) Madhya Pradesh
    (d) Punjab

13. The Pangong lake is situated in ....
    (a) Assam
    (b) Jammu and Kashmir
    (c) Ladakh
    (d) Himachal Pradesh

14. It is the largest salt water lake located in Rajasthan. It is ....
    (a) Sambhar salt lake (b) Chilika lake
    (c) Pushkar lake   (d) Pulicat lake

15. Which among the following is the longest river in the world?
    (a) Nile   (b) Ganga
    (c) Amazon   (d) Yangtze

16. Where is the tallest waterfall (Angel Falls) located in the world?
    (a) France   (b) South Africa
    (c) Zimbabwe   (d) Venezuela

17. Which of the following is the deepest river in the world?
    (a) Amazon   (b) Nile
    (c) Congo   (d) Volga

18. Which of the following rivers carry maximum water into the sea?
    (a) Nile   (b) Amazon
    (c) Congo   (d) Volga

19. Which of the following is a fresh water lake?
    (a) Caspian Sea   (b) Lake Victoria
    (c) Dead Sea   (d) None of these

20. The largest freshwater lake in the world is ....
    (a) Lake Superior (b) Lake Victoria
    (c) Caspian Sea   (d) None of these

2 Marks Questions

21. Find the incorrect pair of cities and rivers.

	Cities		Rivers
(a)	Ludhiyana	–	Sutlej
(b)	Haridwar	–	Ganga
(c)	Nasik	–	Godavari
(d)	Badrinath	–	Ganga

22. Which of the following river originates from a glacier near the holy Mansarovar lake?
    (a) Sutlej
    (b) Indus
    (c) Brahmaputra
    (d) All of the above

23. Which among the following is the Highest Lake in India located at a height of 5,430 metres?
    (a) Pushkar lake
    (b) Gurudongmar lake
    (c) Chilika lake
    (d) Pulicat lake

24. It is the longest lake in India and located in the state of Kerala. This is ....
    (a) Wular lake   (b) Chlika lake
    (c) Vembanad lake (d) Pushkar lake

25. Ahmedabad is situated on the river bank of ....
    (a) Sabarmati   (b) Narmada
    (c) Krishna   (d) Kosi

Chapter
08

Our Environment

1 Mark Questions

1. Which one of the following is NOT a part of sphere present on Earth?
   (a) Lithosphere
   (b) Thermosphere
   (c) Atmosphere
   (d) Hydrosphere

2. Which of the following is not a part of abiotic environment?
   (a) Plants and Animals
   (b) Land and Water
   (c) Air
   (d) None of the above

3. Which of the following would be a biotic factor in an ecosystem?
   (a) Bacteria   (b) Soil
   (c) Temperature   (d) Rainfall

4. Which is the most important gas for our survival?
   (a) Carbon-dioxide (b) Oxygen
   (c) Hydrogen   (d) Nitrogen

5. The most abundant gas present in the atmosphere is ....
   (a) oxygen
   (b) carbon-dioxide
   (c) nitrogen
   (d) hydrogen

6. Which one of the following is the oldest National Park of India?
   (a) Jim Corbett National Park
   (b) Ranthambhore National Park
   (c) Sunderbans National Park
   (d) Gir National Park

7. The Sunderbans Tiger Reserve is located in which State of India?
   (a) Odisha   (b) Maharashtra
   (c) West Bengal   (d) Uttar Pradesh

8. The Gir Forest National Park is known for protection of ....
   (a) Asiatic Lion
   (b) Water Dolphin
   (c) Royal Bengal Tiger
   (d) Cheetah

9. Which of the following activities help us in reducing air pollution?
   (a) Releasing gases from chimneys
   (b) Burning garbage
   (c) Keeping the vehicles off while waiting at the signal
   (d) None of the above

10. Which one of the following is a non-renewable resource?
    (a) Animals   (b) Forests
    (c) Fossil Fuels   (d) Sunlight

11. Renewable sources are the sources ....
    (a) that cannot be reused
    (b) that will never run out
    (c) like Fossil Fuels
    (d) that can be replaced to be used again and again

12. Substances which cause pollution is ....
    (a) polluter
    (b) pollutant
    (c) contaminants
    (d) None of the above

13. Which of the following is biotic component of Biosphere?
    (a) Aur
    (b) Soil
    (c) Water
    (d) Shrubs

14. Sound becomes hazardous noise pollution for human beings at decibels ....
    (a) below 10
    (b) below 20
    (c) below 30
    (d) above 80

15. Which among the following is a poisonous gas present in the atmosphere?
    (a) Carbon-dioxide
    (b) Carbon-monoxide
    (c) Hydrogen
    (d) Nitrogen

16. What is the main reason for the changing of colour of Taj Mahal from white to yellow?
    (a) Deforestation   (b) Afforestation
    (c) Acid rain   (d) None of these

17. Which among the following is an outcome of Global warming?
    (a) Climate change
    (b) Melting of Glaciers
    (c) Deforestation
    (d) Both (a) and (b)

18. Which one of the following is not naturally present on our planet Earth?
    (a) Mountains   (b) Rivers
    (c) Oceans   (d) Petrol

19. Deforestation generally decreases ....
    (a) Rainfall
    (b) Soil erosion
    (c) Global warming
    (d) Weather conditions

20. Ozone layer is being depleted by ....
    (a) Smog
    (b) Chlorofluorocarbon
    (c) Carbon monoxide
    (d) Sulphur dioxide

21. The three R's that will keep our surrounding clean and healthy includes ....
    (a) reduce, reuse and recycle
    (b) reduce, renew and respect
    (c) reuse, repurpose, refuse
    (d) None of the above

2 Marks Questions

22. Which one of the following is the correct food chain system?
(a) Grass --> Grasshopper--> Frog
(b) Tiger --> Deer --> Lion
(c) Snake --> Cat --> Dog
(d) Mouse --> Dog --> Snake

23. Match the following.

List I (Types of Pollution)	List II (Effects of Pollution)
A. Soil pollution	1. Sleep disturbance
B. Air pollution	2. Skin Cancer
C. Water pollution	3. Irritation in the eyes
D. Noise pollution	4. Jaundice

Codes

	A	B	C	D		A	B	C	D
(a)	2	3	4	1	(b)	1	2	3	4
(c)	4	1	2	3	(d)	3	4	1	2

24. Which of the following statement is correct?
1. The ozone layer protects the species of Biosphere from harmful Sun rays.
2. Water and Air pollution causes death of species living in Biosphere.

Codes
(a) Only 1
(b) Only 2
(c) Both 1 and 2
(d) None of the above

25. Which of the following steps can reduce land pollution?
1. Using lesser pesticides.
2. Properly dumping household waste.
3. Using electric vehicle.

Codes
(a) Only 1   (b) Only 2
(c) Both 1 and 2   (d) All of these

Chapter 09

Our Government

1 Mark Questions

1. The Indian Constitution came into effect on ....
   (a) 26th January, 1949
   (b) 26th January, 1950
   (c) 26th January, 1951
   (d) 26th January, 1952

2. The Father of Indian Constitution is ....
   (a) Mahatma Gandhi
   (b) Dr. Rajendra Prasad
   (c) Dr. B.R. Ambedkar
   (d) Dr. S. Radhakrishnan

3. 'We the people of India' is the starting line of ....
   (a) Preamble   (b) National song
   (c) National Motto (d) Constitution

4. Rajya Sabha is also known as .... House of the Parliament.
   (a) Lower   (b) Upper
   (c) Common   (d) None of these

5. Which among the following institutions is responsible for law making?
   (a) Parliament   (b) Supreme Court
   (c) High Court   (d) All of these

6. Who among the following is the real head of the Indian Government?
   (a) President
   (b) Council of Ministers
   (c) Prime Minister
   (d) Governor

7. Who is the 'Supreme Commander' of the Indian armed forces?
   (a) Council of Ministers
   (b) Defence Minister
   (c) President
   (d) Prime Minister

8. The minimum age limit for voting in election is........... .
   (a) 15 years   (b) 18 years
   (c) 19 years   (d) 20 years

9. He/she is the nominal head of the state. Who among the following is this?
   (a) Chief Mminister (b) Chief Justice
   (c) Governor   (d) Civil Servants

10. The President of India is elected for a term of .... years.
    (a) 4   (b) 5   (c) 6   (d) 2

11. Who among the following is appointed as the real head of the state?
    (a) Governor
    (b) Chief Minister
    (c) Chief Secretary
    (d) None of the above

12. The Supreme Court is located in ....
(a) Mumbai (b) Bhopal
(c) New Delhi (d) Bengaluru

13. The Vidhan Sabha and Vidhan Parishad collectively known as ....
(a) Rajya Sabha (b) State Legislature
(c) Lok Sabha (d) None of these

14. Which Judicial body gives the final judgement in any legal case?
(a) Supreme Court of India

(b) High Court
(c) District Court
(d) All of the above

15. It is the highest judicial body in the state. It is ....
(a) Supreme Court (b) High Court
(c) District Court (d) None of these

16. Municipal Corporation is a part of .... local self government.
(a) urban (b) rural
(c) central (d) Both (a) and (b)

2 Marks Questions

17. Which is the lower most level in Panchayati Raj System of India?
(a) Government of State
(b) Governor
(c) Village Panchayat
(d) Municipality

18. Match the following.

Political Party		Symbol of Political Party
A. Indian National Congress	1.	
B. Bhartiya Janata Party	2.	
C. Aam Aadmi Party	3.	
D. Bahujan Samaj Party	4.	

Codes

	A	B	C	D
(a)	3	4	2	1
(b)	4	3	1	2
(c)	3	4	1	2
(d)	1	2	3	4

19. Consider the following statements.
1. The President is the Head of our country.
2. The President of India should be a citizen of India.

Which of the following statements is/are correct?
(a) Only 1 (b) Only 2
(c) Both 1 and 2 (d) None of these

20. Find the mismatched pair
(a) EVM – Voting machine
(b) Head of the state – Governor Government
(c) Panchayati Raj – Rural Development
(d) Minimum age to vote – 25 Years

Chapter 10

General Science

1 Mark Questions

1. It controls your muscles and all organs of the body. It ensures your Heart beats properly. It is ....
   (a) veins   (b) brain
   (c) skin   (d) blood

2. Where in the body most of the digestion takes place?
   (a) Large intestine   (b) Small intestine
   (c) Stomach   (d) Mouth

3. Which organ works as an excretory and a sense organ?
   (a) Lungs   (b) Kidney
   (c) Skin   (d) Ears

4. Pulling away of hand when a hot object is touched is ....
   (a) Reflex action
   (b) Direct action
   (c) Involuntary action
   (d) Sensory action

5. The bones around your chest that protect organs such as the heart are called ....
   (a) Bone marrow   (b) Spine
   (c) Vertebrae   (d) Ribs

6. The Hinge Joint is found in our body in ....
   (a) shoulders   (b) knees
   (c) ankle   (d) wrist

7. Which among the following is an example of immovable joint?
   (a) Arms   (b) Legs
   (c) Jaw line   (d) Wrist

8. The smallest bone in the human body is located in ....
   (a) nose   (b) middle ear
   (c) outer ear   (d) heel

9. .... is the strongest muscle in our body. It is able to heal more quickly than other parts of the body.
   (a) Tongue   (b) Eyes
   (c) Arms   (d) Legs

10. Where in the body new blood cells are made?
   (a) Bone marrow   (b) Heart
   (c) Brain   (d) Kidney

11. It is the only saddle joint in our body. It can move from side to side and back and forth. It is found in ....
   (a) toes   (b) wrist
   (c) thumb   (d) knee

12. .... is known as the 'Body Building' food for our body.
   (a) Fats
   (b) Protein
   (c) Carbohydrates
   (d) Vitamins and Minerals

13. Deficiency of Iron causes ....
(a) Rickets   (b) Malnutrition
(c) Anaemia   (d) Goitre

14. Eating too much fatty food and oily food leads to ....
(a) Obesity
(b) High Blood Pressure
(c) Typhoid
(d) Diabetes

15. Select the deficiency that causes loss of bone density and which increases the risk of fractures.
(a) Vitamin C   (b) Vitamin D
(c) Vitamin A   (d) Vitamin B

16. Night Blindness is caused due to lack of ....
(a) Vitamin C   (b) Vitamin D
(c) Vitamin A   (d) Vitamin B

17. Which among the following is not a function of roots?
(a) They provide support to the plant.
(b) They absorb water and nutrients from the soil.
(c) They bear branches, leaves and fruits.
(d) They hold the soil firmly.

18. Plants with green and soft stem like mint, rosemary are examples of ....
(a) Shrubs   (b) Climbers
(c) Herbs   (d) Creepers

19. Creepers are plants with weak stems. One of the examples of this is ....
(a) money plant   (b) rose
(c) watermelon   (d) mint

20. The food factory or kitchen of the plant is ....
(a) root   (b) stem
(c) flower   (d) leaves

21. Which plant store food in their stem?
(a) Potato   (b) Watermelon
(c) Tomato   (d) Lemon

22. The condition needed for germination of seed includes ....
(a) air   (b) water
(c) right temperature (d) All of these

23. To which category does the bird shown in the given image belong?

(a) Herbivores   (b) Carnivores
(c) Omnivores   (d) None of these

24. Whales breathe through their ....
(a) gills   (b) skin
(c) lungs   (d) nostril

25. Which of the following statements is incorrect?
(a) Dolphins do not have lungs.
(b) The thick fur of Polar bears keeps them warm in cold weather.
(c) Whale has to come up to the surface water to breathe.
(d) Birds migrate during the winter season.

26. Amphibians live both on land and water. One of the examples of this is ....
(a) snake   (b) frog
(c) turtle   (d) tiger

27. Which of these animals uses flippers for its movement?
(a) Penguin   (b) Frog
(c) Lizard   (d) Tortoise

28. Which among the following is the only mammal which can fly?
    (a) Bats   (b) Ostrich
    (c) Flamingo   (d) None of these

29. Which of the following animals is a reptile?
    (a) Snake   (b) Frog
    (c) Dolphin   (d) Penguin

30. Ice-cream melts when energy in the form of .... is supplied.
    (a) sound   (b) heat
    (c) wind   (d) light

31. Which would be the best material for making the handle of Tea Kettle?
    (a) Copper   (b) Aluminium
    (c) Steel   (d) Plastic

32. The forces of attraction between the molecules are strongest in the state of ....
    (a) solid   (b) liquid
    (c) gas   (d) Both (a) and (b)

33. A substance which allows light to pass through it and can break easily is......... .
    (a) iron rod   (b) glass
    (c) ceramic tile   (d) paper

34. Which process converts liquid to gaseous state?
    (a) Condensation   (b) Evaporation
    (c) Boiling   (d) Melting

35. Butter paper is a/an .... object.
    (a) transparent object
    (b) translucent object
    (c) opaque object
    (d) None of the above

36. Squeezing of lemon and writing in our notebooks are examples of which kind of force?
    (a) Gravitational Force
    (b) Muscular Force
    (c) Magnetic Force
    (d) Frictional Force

37. Things fall on the ground due to .... force.
    (a) muscular   (b) frictional
    (c) magnetic   (d) gravitational

38. The direction of frictional force is always ....
    (a) normal to the direction of motion of an object
    (b) in the direction of an object
    (c) opposite to the direction of motion of an object
    (d) at an angle (90 degree) to the direction of motion of an object

39. Smoother surfaces will have ....
    (a) more friction
    (b) less friction
    (c) same level of friction
    (d) no friction

40. Shadows are longer during ....
    (a) evening   (b) afternoon
    (c) morning   (d) Both (b) and (c)

41. The famous scientist who discovered gravity is................. .
    (a) Albert Einstein
    (b) Issac Newton
    (c) Michael Faraday
    (d) None of the above

42. Who among the following gave the Theory of Relativity?
    (a) Issac Newton
    (b) Thomas Edison
    (c) Albert Einstein
    (d) Alexander Graham Bell

43. Who is known as the inventor of the Steam Engine?
    (a) Thomas Edison (b) James Watt
    (c) Graham Bell   (d) Copernicus

2 Marks Questions

44. State True (T) or False (F) for the given statements.

    A. Bones are connected to each other through ligaments.

    B. For healthy digestion, avoid overeating.

    C. Elbows and knees can move in all directions

    D. Heart muscles work in the body even when we sleep.

Codes

	A	B	C	D		A	B	C	D
(a)	T	F	T	F	(b)	T	T	F	T
(c)	T	T	F	F	(d)	F	F	T	T

45. The Food items given in the image help us to fight from germs and diseases. They are known as Protective Foods. They are a source of ....

(a) protein
(b) fats
(c) carbohydrates
(d) vitamins and minerals

46. A ship is heavier than iron nail, but floats on the water surface, while nail sinks because................. .

(a) iron nail is small and ship is big in size.
(b) weight of ship becomes equal to the weight of water it displaces.
(c) ship has large surface area than iron nail.
(d) None of the above

47. In a thunderstorm, light reaches first to the Earth's surface than sound because ....

(a) speed of light is much more than the speed of sound
(b) speed of sound is equal to speed of light
(c) speed of sound is more than speed of light
(d) None of the above

48. Match the following.

List I (Name of Body Parts)		List II (Organ System)
A. Stomach	1.	Excretory System
B. Kidneys	2.	Circulatory System
C. Lungs	3.	Respiratory System
D. Heart	4.	Skeleton System
E. Spinal Cord	5.	Digestive System

Codes

	A	B	C	D	E
(a)	1	3	2	5	4
(b)	5	1	3	2	4
(c)	2	3	4	1	5
(d)	3	5	1	2	4

49. Match the following.

List I (Types of Teeth)	List II (Uses of Teeth)
A. Incisors	1. Grinding
B. Canines	2. Cracking
C. Premolars	3. Cutting
D. Molars	4. Tearing

Codes

	A	B	C	D		A	B	C	D
(a)	3	4	2	1	(b)	4	3	1	2
(c)	2	1	3	4	(d)	1	2	4	3

Computers

1 Mark Questions

1. Fifth generation computers are based on ....
   (a) Artificial Intelligence
   (b) Programmed Instruction
   (c) Nanotechnology
   (d) Bioinformatics

2. Which among the following is both input and output device?
   (a) 
   (b)
   (c)
   (d)

3. This part sends signals to other parts of the computer to tell them what to do. It is ....
   (a) Central Processing Unit
   (b) Motherboard
   (c) Hard drive
   (d) Monitor

4. This memory is for short term storage and is lost when computer is turned off. It is ....
   (a) Memory Card   (b) Hard drive
   (c) RAM   (d) Flash Drive

5. It is an image representing a folder or a program. This is ....
   (a) Application software
   (b) Icon
   (c) Graphic
   (d) All of the above

6. Another name for computer programs and information is ....
   (a) Software
   (b) Hardware
   (c) Technology
   (d) User Interface

7. .... is a combination of hardware and software that facilitates the sharing of information between computing devices.
   - (a) Network
   - (b) Digital Device
   - (c) Modem
   - (d) Compiler

8. CD-ROM stands for ....
   - (a) Compactable Read Only Memory
   - (b) Compactable Disk Read Only Memory
   - (c) Compact Disk–Read Only Memory
   - (d) Compact Data Read Only Memory

9. Microsoft Word is an example of which Software?
   - (a) System software
   - (b) Operating system
   - (c) Application software
   - (d) None of the above

10. Which of the following computer program can be used to make spreadsheets?
    - (a) MS Word
    - (b) Adope Reader
    - (c) MS Excel
    - (d) Google Chrome

11. The 0 and 1 in the Binary numbering system are called Binary digits as well as ....
    - (a) Bytes
    - (b) Kilobytes
    - (c) Bits
    - (d) Decimal Bytes

12. A collection of 8 bits is called ....
    - (a) Byte
    - (b) Word
    - (c) Kilobytes
    - (d) None of these

13. A Kilobyte is also referred as KB is equal to ....
    - (a) 1000 bytes
    - (b) 1024 bytes
    - (c) 512 bytes
    - (d) 1224 bytes

14. Which of the following is the most powerful type of computer?
    - (a) Mainframe
    - (b) Micro Computer
    - (c) Super Computer
    - (d) Mini Computer

15. One of the advantages of using computer is that ....
    - (a) they produce accurate information.
    - (b) they are very fast and can store huge amount of data.
    - (c) they are designed to be inflexible.
    - (d) All of the above

16. The process of removing unwanted part of an image is called ....
    - (a) Hiding
    - (b) Cropping
    - (c) Editing
    - (d) Formatting

17. To apply center alignment to a paragraph we can press ....
    - (a) Ctrl + A
    - (b) Ctrl + S
    - (c) Ctrl + E
    - (d) Ctrl + V

18. In which view, Headers and Footers are visible?
    - (a) Normal view
    - (b) Page Layout view
    - (c) Print Layout view
    - (d) Draft view

19. To spell check which function key will you press?
    - (a) F5
    - (b) F6
    - (c) F7
    - (d) F8

20. The Tabs that appear at the bottom of each workbook is called ....
    - (a) Location Tabs
    - (b) Sheet Tabs
    - (c) Reference Tabs
    - (d) None of the above

21. We can send MS Word documents to which of the following?
    - (a) MS Excel
    - (b) MS Access
    - (c) MS PowerPoint
    - (d) All of the above

22. What is the maximum number of columns that can be inserted in a Word Document?

(a) 45   (b) 50

(c) 55   (d) 63

23. In MS Excel which toolbar allows you to enter values and formulas?

(a) Title Bar

(b) Formula Bar

(c) Standard Toolbar

(d) Menu Bar

2 Marks Questions

24. By mistake you deleted a record in the Excel sheet. Which command can be used to restore the data immediately?

(a) Ctrl + V   (b) Ctrl + Z

(c) Ctrl + S   (d) Ctrl + O

25. Which type of charts can Excel produce?

(a) Only Line graphs

(b) Bar charts, Line graphs and Pie charts

(c) Bar charts and Pie charts only

(d) None of the above

26. What is the smallest and largest font available on Formatting Toolbar?

(a) Smallest- 8 and Largest- 70

(b) Smallest- 6 and Largest- 72

(c) Smallest- 10 and Largest-74

(d) Smallest- 8 and Largest- 72

27. Shortcut key for the Slide Show view is ....

(a) F1   (b) F3

(c) F5   (d) F4

28. Which of the following pair is matched correctly?

(a) System Software–MS Windows

(b) Application Software–Google Chrome

(c) Utility software–Antivirus Program

(d) All of the above

General Knowledge

Superlatives in India and World

1. Which is the most populous city in the world?
   (a) Delhi   (b) Beijing
   (c) Tokyo   (d) New York

2. Which is the highest mountain peak in the world?
   (a) K2
   (b) Mount Everest
   (c) Alps
   (d) Mount Kilimanjaro

3. The largest hot desert in the world is .... present in Africa.
   (a) Gibson   (b) Sahara
   (c) Gobi   (d) Thar

4. Which among the following is the biggest and coldest desert in Asia?
   (a) Thar Desert
   (b) Gobi Desert
   (c) Kalahari Desert
   (d) None of the above

5. The world's longest bridge is ....
   (a) Kunshan Grand bridge
   (b) Golden Gate bridge
   (c) Brooklyn bridge
   (d) Sydney Harbour bridge

6. Which is the largest Island of the world?
   (a) Iceland   (b) Greenland
   (c) Madagascar   (d) None of these

7. Which among the following is the largest railway platform in the world?
   (a) Chicago Union Station, Chicago
   (b) Lahore Junction, Pakistan
   (c) Chhatrapati Shivaji Terminus, Mumbai
   (d) Grand Central Terminal, New York

8. Which is the biggest fish in the world?
   (a) Dolphin   (b) Catfish
   (c) Star fish   (d) Whale shark

9. Which of the following is the largest airport in India?
   (a) Chennai International Airport
   (b) Indira Gandhi International Airport
   (c) Chhatrapati Shivaji Maharaj International Airport
   (d) Rajiv Gandhi International Airport

10. The longest bridge in India is
   (a) Howrah bridge
   (b) Dhola-Sadiya Bridge
   (c) Atal bridge
   (d) Golden bridge

11. It is the largest bird on the Earth. This is
....
(a) Humming Bird   (b) Ostrich
(c) Woodpecker   (d) Owl

12. Which among the following is the smallest bird on the Earth?
(a) Woodpecker   (b) Parrot
(c) Humming Bird   (d) Owl

Countries, Capitals, Currencies, Flags and Nicknames

13. Which country is called the 'Land of Golden Fibre'?
(a) Sri Lanka   (b) Bangladesh
(c) Maldives   (d) Nepal

14. Which of the given combinations of country and currency are incorrect?
(a) Belgium – Euro
(b) Portugal – Dollar
(c) Thailand– Baht
(d) Chile – Peso

15. Identify the country which is famous for its technological advancements
(a) North Korea   (b) South Korea
(c) China   (d) Japan

16. Identify the country from the flag shown below

(a) Turkey   (b) Zimbabwe
(c) South Africa   (d) Canada

17. Which of the following country's flag is similar to that of India interms of its stripes of colours?
(a) Germany   (b) France
(c) Niger   (d) Australia

18. How many states have joined together to form the United States of America?
(a) Twenty   (b) Fifty
(c) Sixty   (d) Ten

19. Which country is known as The Pearl of Indian Ocean?
(a) Myammar
(b) Sri Lanka
(c) Madagascar
(d) India

20. Which country is popularly known as the Rainbow Nation?
(a) USA   (b) Japan
(c) China   (d) South Africa

21. The capital of Netherlands is ....
(a) Wellington   (b) Ottawa
(c) Amsterdam   (d) Oslo

22. .... is the capital of Malaysia.
(a) Port Louis   (b) Kuala Lumpur
(c) Seoul   (d) Stockholm

23. Abu Dhabi is the capital city of which country?
(a) Iran
(b) Iraq
(c) United Arab Emirates
(d) Mauritius

24. Which of the following countries has it's capital name same as country's name?
(a) Singapore   (b) Macau
(c) Vatican City   (d) All of these

25. Russia is the largest country in the world, which is the second largest?
    (a) India   (b) China
    (c) Australia   (d) Canada

26. Which of the following countries has three capitals?
    (a) India   (b) Australia
    (c) South Africa   (d) Japan

27. Find the incorrect pair of countries and capitals given below.
    (a) Italy – Rome
    (b) Kuwait – Kuwait city
    (c) Saudi Arabia – Kabul
    (d) Nepal – Kathmandu

28. Find the odd one out.
    (a) France   (b) Italy
    (c) Portugal   (d) Brazil

29. What is the currency of Spain?
    (a) Pound   (b) Dollar
    (c) Euro   (d) Krona

30. Which country is popularly known as 'The Land of Free'?
    (a) Brazil   (b) Bangladesh
    (c) United States of America
    (d) New Zealand

31. Which country is known as 'Land of White Elephant'?
    (a) South Africa   (b) India
    (c) Thailand   (d) Sri Lanka

32. Which country is called 'Heart of Europe'?
    (a) Holland   (b) Poland
    (c) Germany   (d) Netherlands

33. Which country is called 'Crossroads of Europe'?
    (a) Canada   (b) France
    (c) Germany   (d) Belgium

34. Which of the following country lies in Europe as well as Asia?
    (a) Germany   (b) Afghanistan
    (c) Russia   (d) Egypt

35. Which of the following cities is known as 'City of Canals'?
    (a) Paris   (b) Amsterdam
    (c) Venice   (d) London

36. Which city of the world is popularly known as Big Apple?
    (a) London   (b) Rome
    (c) Barcelona   (d) New York

37. The oldest city in the world is in ....
    (a) Oslo, Norway
    (b) Damascus, Syria
    (c) New York, United States
    (d) London, United Kingdom

38. Which is the world's second most populous city of the world?
    (a) Beijing   (b) Tokyo
    (c) London   (d) Mexico

39. Which city is called 'Golden City of India'?
    (a) Udaipur   (b) Jodhpur
    (c) Jaisalmer   (d) Jaipur

40. Which city is popularly known as 'Queen of Arabian Sea'?
    (a) Chennai   (b) Mumbai
    (c) Mussorie   (d) Kochi

41. 'The diamond and textile city' of India is ....
    (a) Lucknow   (b) Meerut
    (c) Surat   (d) Trivandrum

42. This city is known as 'City of Pearls'. It is ....
    (a) Hyderabad   (b) Jaipur
    (c) Jodhpur   (d) Jamshedpur

43. Temple city of India is ....
  (a) Jaipur (b) Jamshedpur
  (c) Bhubaneswar (d) Kannauj

44. Match the following.

List I (Name of Country)	List II (Currency Symbol)
A. Japan	1. ₽ (Ruble)
B. Italy	2. £ (Pound)
C. United Kingdom	3. ¥ (Yen)
D. Russia	4. £ (Lira)

Codes

	A	B	C	D		A	B	C	D
(a)	3	4	2	1	(b)	4	3	1	2
(c)	2	3	4	1	(d)	1	2	3	4

45. Match the following.

List I (Capital)	List II (Name of the country)
A. Dhaka	1. Israel
B. Jerusalem	2. Mauritius
C. Port Louis	3. Afghanistan
D. Kabul	4. Bangladesh

Codes

	A	B	C	D
(a)	3	4	1	2
(b)	4	1	2	3
(c)	2	3	1	4
(d)	1	2	3	4

National Symbols and Languages

46. In the Indian National Flag, Saffron represents ....
  (a) Peace (b) Truth
  (c) Courage (d) Prosperity

47. Which of the following animals are present in the National Emblem of India?
  (a) Horse
  (b) Bull
  (c) Lion
  (d) All of the above

48. The word 'Satyamev Jayate' on the State Emblem means ....
  (a) Truth shall live on
  (b) Only truth prevails
  (c) Truth will triumph
  (d) Truth will be served

49. National Heritage animal of India is ....
  (a) Elephant
  (b) Rhinoceros
  (c) Tiger
  (d) Lion

50. The National Tree of India is associated with longevity and has important medicinal properties. It is ....
  (a) Curry Tree
  (b) Banyan Tree
  (c) Dragon Tree
  (d) Cacao Tree

51. The language with the richest vocabulary is ....
  (a) Hindi (b) Sanskrit
  (c) English (d) French

52. Telugu is spoken in which state of India?
    (a) Kerala
    (b) Andhra Pradesh
    (c) Karnataka
    (d) Tamil Nadu

53. Sanskrit is official language of the state ....
    (a) Delhi
    (b) Tamil Nadu
    (c) Uttarakhand
    (d) Himachal Pradesh

54. Second most spoken language in India after Hindi is ....
    (a) English   (b) Tamil
    (c) Bengali   (d) Punjabi

55. Which of the following countries has the greatest number of official languages?
    (a) India
    (b) China
    (c) USA
    (d) Russia

56. Which among the following languages is the most spoken language in the world?
    (a) English   (b) French
    (c) Chinese   (d) German

57. Dogri language is spoken by the people of which region?
    (a) Goa
    (b) Jammu and Kashmir
    (c) Meghalaya
    (d) Sikkim

Books and Authors

1. The only religious book ever printed in a short hand scripts is............ .
   (a) the Ramayana
   (b) the Mahabharata
   (c) the Bible
   (d) Guru Granth Sahib

2. The book 'You are Born to Blossom' is written by which author?
   (a) Chetan Bhagat
   (b) APJ Abdul Kalam
   (c) Mahatma Gandhi
   (d) Pranab Mukherjee

3. Which among the following books is a treatise on economics and politics written by Chanakya?
   (a) Arthashastra
   (b) Natyashastra
   (c) Bhugolshastra
   (d) None of these

4. The book 'Discovery of India' was authored by ....
   (a) Mahatma Gandhi
   (b) Jawaharlal Nehru
   (c) Sardar Vallabhbhai Patel
   (d) Rajiv Gandhi

5. The book 'Seven lecrets of Shiva' is written by which famous mythologist?
   (a) Amish Tripathi
   (b) Devdutt Pattanaik
   (c) Chitra Banerjee
   (d) None of the above

6. The 'Long Walk to Freedom' is the autobiography of ....
   (a) Bill Clinton
   (b) George Bush
   (c) Nelson Mandela
   (d) Martin Luther King Jr.

7. Who among the following was a 'Sanskrit poet' known as Indian Shakespeare?
   (a) Kautilya
   (b) Kalidasa
   (c) Surdas
   (d) Tulsidas

8. The story 'Swami and Friends' was written by which novelist?
   (a) Ruskin Bond
   (b) Vikram Seth
   (c) Shashi Tharoor
   (d) RK Narayan

9. The book 'Straight from Heart' is the biography of which cricketer?
   (a) Yuvraj Singh
   (b) Kapil Dev
   (c) Rohit Sharma
   (d) Sachin Tendulkar

10. Who among the following is the author of 'Two States'?
    (a) Chetan Bhagat   (b) Arundhati Roy
    (c) Vikram Seth   (d) Jhumpa Lahiri

11. The book 'Race of My Life' is the biography of which of the following?
    (a) Hima Das   (b) Ussain Bolt
    (c) Milkha Singh   (d) Neeraj Chopra

12. Which of the following sportspersons wrote the autobiographical book 'Ace Against Odds'?
    (a) Mary Kom   (b) Saina Nehwal
    (c) Sania Mirza   (d) P.V. Sindhu

13. Rabindranath Tagore received Novel price in literature for which of the following books?
    (a) Kabuliwala   (b) Gitanjali
    (c) My Gita   (d) We The People

14. The character Sherlock Holmes, a famous detective, was created by which author?
    (a) JK Rowling
    (b) Arthur Doyle
    (c) Walt Disney
    (d) Vikarm Seth

15. Match the following.

List I (Name of Authors)	List II (Name of Books)
A. Munshi Premchand	1. Bhagvad Gita
B. Ved Vyasa	2. Maalgudi Ki Kahaniyan
C. R.K. Narayan	3. Geetanjali
D. Rabindranath Tagore	4. Godaan

Codes

	A	B	C	D
(a)	4	1	2	3
(b)	3	2	1	4
(c)	1	3	4	2
(d)	4	3	2	1

Chapter

14

Important Days and Dates

1 Mark Questions

1. The birth anniversary of Swami Vivekananda is celebrated as ....
(a) National Voter's Day
(b) National Youth Day
(c) Army Day
(d) National Science Day

2. Every year 'Human Rights Day' is held on ....
(a) 5th December   (b) 7th December
(c) 9th December   (d) 10th December

3. Which of the following days are celebrated on 25th January?
(a) National Tourism Day
(b) National Voters Day
(c) World Hindi Day
(d) Both (a) and (b)

4. National Engineer's Day is celebrated in India to pay tribute to which personality?
(a) CV Raman   (b) M Visvesvaraya
(c) Homi Bhabha   (d) None of these

5. On 28th January the birth anniversary of a prominent nationalist leader is celebrated. He was also known as 'Lion of Punjab.' This day is ....
(a) Birth anniversary of Lala Lajpat Rai
(b) Birth anniversary of Bhagat Singh

(c) Birth anniversary of Chandra Shekhar Azad
(d) Birth anniversary of Bal Gangadhar Tilak

6. Which date is observed as Martyr's Day in the memory of Mahatma Gandhi?
(a) 27th January
(b) 28th January
(c) 30th January
(d) 31st January

7. On 13th of April every year, which historical day is observed in the memory of those who were killed in that incident?
(a) Jallianwala Bagh Massacre Day
(b) Anti-Sikh riots
(c) Great revolt of 1857
(d) Anti-Muslim riots

8. In what way, 14th of November is celebrated in India?
(a) As a tribute to our first Prime Minister.
(b) To increase awareness on the rights and education of children.
(c) It is a birth anniversary of Jawaharlal Nehru.
(d) All of the above

9. On which date the World Environment Day is observed?
   (a) 5th May   (b) 5th June
   (c) 5th July   (d) 5th August

10. International Girl Child Day is celebrated across the world on ....
    (a) 9th October
    (b) 10th October
    (c) 11th October
    (d) 12th October

11. World Population Day, to raise awareness about Global population problems is celebrated on
    (a) 9th July   (b) 10th July
    (c) 11th July   (d) 12th July

12. World Nature Conservation Day is held every year on ....
    (a) 26th July   (b) 27th July
    (c) 28th July   (d) 29th July

13. The National Sports Day is celebrated in India as a tribute to major Dhyan Chand. It is celebrated on ....
    (a) 29th August
    (b) 30th August
    (c) 31st August
    (d) 1st September

14. International Day of Non-violence is observed on ....
    (a) 1st October
    (b) 2nd October
    (c) 3rd October
    (d) 4th October

15. Every year "World Peace Day" is celebrated by United Nations on ....
    (a) 1st January
    (b) 2nd January
    (c) 21 September
    (d) 5th January

2 Marks Questions

16. Match the following.

List I (Important Days)		List II (Observed On)
A.	World Laughter Day	1. 28th February
B.	Indian Army Day	2. 10th January
C.	World Cancer Day	3. 15th January
D.	National Science Day	4. 4th February

Codes

	A	B	C	D
(a)	1	2	3	4
(b)	2	3	4	1
(c)	3	4	2	1
(d)	4	3	1	2

17. State T for (True) and F for (False) for the given statements.
    1. International Women's Day is observed on 8th February.
    2. International Day of Happiness is held on 20 March.
    3. On 20th March, World Water Day is celebrated.
    4. On 7th April, World Health Day is observed.

	1	2	3	4
(a)	T	F	T	F
(b)	T	T	F	T
(c)	T	F	F	T
(d)	F	T	T	F

18. Match the following.

Important Days	Observed On
A. International Labour Day	1. 12th August
B. World Wildlife Day	2. 15th May
C. International Day of Family	3. 3rd March
D. World Youth Day	4. 1st May

Codes

	A	B	C	D		A	B	C	D
(a)	1	2	3	4	(b)	2	3	4	1
(c)	4	3	2	1	(d)	3	4	1	2

19. Which of the following statements is/are true?

1. 'National Science Day' is celebrated in India as a tribute to CV Raman.

2. 'World Heart Day' is celebrated every year on 29th September to spread awareness about Heart Health.

Codes
(a) Only 1
(b) Only 2
(c) Both 1 and 2
(d) None of the above

20. Select the pair which is matched correctly?

Days	Celebration
(a) National Girl Child Day	— 11th October
(b) World AIDS Day	— 1st December
(c) Christmas Day	— 5th December
(d) World Labour Day	— 1st January

Chapter 15

Awards and Honours

1 Mark Questions

1. 'Nobel Prizes' are not given for which of the following fields?
   (a) Physics and Chemistry
   (b) Language and Economics
   (c) Peace and Social Work
   (d) Music and Mathematics

2. The First Asian (Indian) to receive Nobel Prize is ....
   (a) Rabindranath Tagore
   (b) C.V. Raman
   (c) Amartya Sen
   (d) Mother Teresa

3. Who among the following was the first Indian woman to receive Nobel Peace Prize?
   (a) Kasturba Gandhi
   (b) Indira Gandhi
   (c) Mother Teresa
   (d) None of the above

4. The youngest person awarded with the Nobel Prize at the age of 17 years is ....
   (a) Kailash Satyarthi
   (b) Malala Yousafzai
   (c) Lawrence Bragg
   (d) Betty Williams

5. Bharat Ratna, Padma Vibhushan and Padma Shree are given on the event of
   (a) Republic Day   (b) Independence Day
   (c) Vijaya Diwas   (d) Gandhi Jayanti

6. Who selects the awardees for Padma Awards?
   (a) President of India
   (b) Prime Minister of India
   (c) A selected committee for the award
   (d) Both (a) and (b)

7. Who among the following was/were the first recipients of Bharat Ratna Award in 1954?
   (a) C.V. Raman
   (b) Sarvepalli Radhakrishnan
   (c) C. Rajagopalachari
   (d) All of the above

8. In which field Dada Saheb Phalke Award is given?
   (a) Literature   (b) Film
   (c) Sports   (d) Science

9. Which of the following is the highest gallantry award of India?
   (a) Mahavir Chakra (b) Param Vir Chakra
   (c) Ashok Chakra   (d) Vir Chakra

10. Which of the following is India's highest peace-time gallantry award?
    (a) Mahavir Chakra (b) Vir Chakra
    (c) Ashok Chakra (d) Param Vir Chakra

11. National Bravery Awards are given to brave children on which event?
    (a) Republic Day
    (b) Gandhi Jayanti
    (c) Independence Day
    (d) Children's Day

12. National Bravery Award consists of how many categories of Awards?
    (a) 4 (b) 5
    (c) 6 (d) 7

13. Who got the First National Bravery Award?
    (a) Harish Chandra
    (b) Gunjan Sharma
    (c) Rajdeep Das
    (d) Muhammed Muhsin

2 Marks Questions

14. The Academy Awards, popularly known as ...., are awards for artistic and technical merit in the film industry.

    (a) The Oscars
    (b) Golden Globe
    (c) IIFA
    (d) National Film Awards

15. Consider the following statements.
    1. Rajiv Gandhi Khel Ratna Award is the highest honour given in sports.
    2. It is given to the best Coach in India.

Which of the following statements is/are correct?
(a) Only 1 (b) Only 2
(c) Both 1 and 2 (d) Neither1 nor 2

16. Which of the given pair is correctly matched?
    1. Arjuna Award– Sports and Games
    2. Grammy Award – Music Industry
    3. Jnanapith Award – Drama And Acting

    Codes
    (a) Only 1 and 2 (b) Only 2 and 3
    (c) Only 1 and 3 (d) All of these

17. Which of the pair given below is matched correctly?
    1. Shaurya Chakra–Military Award
    2. Padma Bhushan– Civilian Award
    3. Dronacharya Award–Sports Award

    Codes
    (a) Only 1 and 2 (b) Only 2 and 3
    (c) Only 1 and 3 (d) All of these

Sports

1 Mark Questions

1. The five rings on Olympic flag represents
....
   (a) five games
   (b) five colours
   (c) five continents
   (d) five countries

2. Identify the sports personality from the given image.

   Hint : She is a Russian Tennis player and is also an Olympic medal list.

   (a) Maria Sharapova
   (b) Serena Williams
   (c) Naomi Osaka
   (d) Steffi Graf

3. Serena Williams is one of the top ranked sportswomen of ....
   (a) Table Tennis   (b) Tennis
   (c) Badminton   (d) Golf

4. How many team members are there on each side of a Kabaddi match?
   (a) 5   (b) 6
   (c) 7   (d) 8

5. Which is the governing body for the sport of Archery?
   (a) World Archery Federation
   (b) World Archery Association
   (c) World Archery Council
   (d) Archery Federation of World

6. Who has won the ICC World Cup the most number of times?
   (a) Sri Lanka
   (b) India
   (c) Australia
   (d) South Africa

7. Which Indian player won the first Olympic Gold in Shooting?
   (a) Abhinav Bindra
   (b) Gagan Narang
   (c) Rajyavardhan Singh Rathore
   (d) Jitu Rai

8. Who among the following became the First Grandmaster from India?
   (a) Viswanathan Anand
   (b) Soumya Swaminathan
   (c) Subbaraman Vijayalakshmi
   (d) Pentala Harikrishna

9. What is the shape of the Basketball Field?
   (a) Oval
   (b) Square
   (c) Rectangular
   (d) Circular

10. Which of the following terms is not associated with Football?
    (a) Catch
    (b) Penalty Kick
    (c) Off Side
    (d) Penalty Stroke

11. Which of the following country won Football World Cup maximum times?
    (a) Germany
    (b) Brazil
    (c) Argentina
    (d) Italy

12. The asana shown in the image is ………

    (a) Bhujangasana
    (b) Sukhasana
    (c) Vrikshasana
    (d) Tadasan

13. Identify the Yoga asana given in the image below.

    (a) Tadasana (Mountain Pose)
    (b) Vrikshasana (Tree Pose)
    (c) Naukasana (Boat Pose)
    (d) Bhujangasana (Cobra Pose)

14. Which of the following stadiums is associated with Hockey?
    (a) Eden Garden Stadium
    (b) Sardar Patel Stadium
    (c) Dhyan Chand Stadium
    (d) Nehru Stadium

15. Which is the only player allowed to touch the ball with his feet during a Hockey match?
    (a) Defender
    (b) Goal keeper
    (c) Centre-Forward
    (d) None of the above

16. Which is known as the oldest sports in the world?
    (a) Tennis
    (b) Cricket
    (c) Wrestling
    (d) Football

17. She is the first female wrestler to win Gold medal in Commonwealth games. Identify the sports personality from the given image.

    (a) Babita Phogat
    (b) Geeta Phogat
    (c) Priyanka Phogat
    (d) Ritu Phogat

18. How many times can a player strike a shuttlecock before it flies over the net?
    (a) Once
    (b) Twice
    (c) Thrice
    (d) None of the above

19. Who was the first Indian badminton player to hold number one rank in world ranking?
(a) Saina Nehwal
(b) Prakash Padukone
(c) Chetan Anand
(d) P.V. Sindhu

20. Who won India's first Olympic Medal in badminton?
(a) Saina Nehwal
(b) P.V. Sindhu
(c) Jwala Gutta
(d) Ashwini Ponnappa

21. Who among the following is nicknamed as "Dhing Express"?
(a) Swapna Barman
(b) Hima Das
(c) P. T. Usha
(d) Dutee Chand

22. Who is the first Indian woman to win Asian games Gold in 400m run?
(a) Kamaljit Sandhu
(b) Dutee Chand
(c) Tintu Luka
(d) Rita Sen

2 Marks Questions

23. Match the following.

List I (Name of Cricket Stadium)		List II (Location)
A.	Wankhede Stadium	1. Ahmedabad
B.	Sardar Patel Stadium	2. Delhi
C.	Eden Gardens	3. Mumbai
D.	Arun Jaitely Stadium	4. Kolkata

Codes

	A	B	C	D			A	B	C	D
(a)	1	2	3	4	(b)		4	3	2	1
(c)	3	1	4	2	(d)		2	4	1	3

24. Match the following.

List I (Name of Country)		List II (National Sports)
A.	USA	1. Table Tennis
B.	United Kingdom	2. Bull Fighting
C.	Spain	3. Baseball
D.	China	4. Cricket

Codes

	A	B	C	D
(a)	1	2	3	4
(b)	2	3	1	4
(c)	3	4	2	1
(d)	4	3	2	1

25. Match the following.

List I (Player)		List II (Sports)
A.	Prithvi Shaw	1. Cricket
B.	Arjun Kalyan	2. Badminton
C.	PV Sindhu	3. Hockey
D.	Sardara Singh	4. Chess

Codes

	A	B	C	D
(a)	2	3	4	1
(b)	1	4	2	3
(c)	1	2	3	4
(d)	2	4	1	3

PRACTICE SET 

1. Nobel Prizes are not given for which of the following fields ?
   (a) Physics   (b) Chemistry
   (c) Peace   (d) Music

2. Which one of the following instruments is used to connect our personal computer with internet?
   (a) USB
   (b) Modem
   (c) Pen drive
   (d) Telephone

3. Which of the following is not an operating system?
   (a) Android   (b) Windows
   (c) Linux   (d) Java

4. The 'Dronacharya Award' is associated with ....
   (a) Eminent Surgeons
   (b) Famous Artists
   (c) Sport Coaches
   (d) Expert Engineers

5. Which one of the following term is related with the Prime Minister of India?
   (a) Head of the Government
   (b) Head of the state
   (c) Head of India
   (d) FIrst citizen of India

6. Which of the following is a form of martial arts?
   (a) Judo   (b) Kung fu
   (c) Karate   (d) All of these

7. Which among the following planets have no moon?
   (a) Neptune
   (b) Venus
   (c) Mercury
   (d) Pluto

8. Which book among the following is written by Munshi Premchand?
   (a) Geetanjali   (b) Parineeta
   (c) The Post Office   (d) Idgah

9. The path which Earth makes around the Sun is called the ....
   (a) axis
   (b) rotation
   (c) counterclockwise
   (d) orbit

10. Which mughal emperor built the Agra fort?
    (a) Babur   (b) Shah Jahan
    (c) Humayun   (d) Akbar

11. Which of the following is a renewable source of energy?
    (a) Solar Energy
    (b) Wind Energy
    (c) Hydro Energy
    (d) All of the above

12. India won the first Cricket World Cup in the year ....
    (a) 1975   (b) 1983
    (c) 1979   (d) 1987

13. Which among the following rivers is the longest river of the world?
    (a) Amazon   (b) Nile
    (c) Yamuna   (d) Ravi

14. The holy book 'Ramcharitmanas' was writtten by ....
    (a) Tulsidas   (b) Valmiki
    (c) Surdas   (d) Ved Vyas

15. Which among the following lake is located in Jammu and Kashmir?
    (a) Chilika lake   (b) Wular lake
    (c) Loktak lake   (d) Vemband lake

16. Which one of the famous kings succeeded Chandragupt Maurya?
    (a) Ashoka   (b) Kanishka
    (c) Bindusara   (d) Bimbisara

17. Which of the following freedom fighter is also known as Prince of Patriots?
    (a) Mahatma Gandhi
    (b) Bhagat Singh
    (c) Subhash Chandra Bose
    (d) Sukhdev

18. Which among the following is the longest dam present in India?
    (a) Tehri Dam
    (b) Hirakud Dam
    (c) Bhakra Nangal Dam
    (d) Tungbhadra Dam

19. Which of the following day is celebrated to honour the discovery of Raman Effect by CV Raman?
    (a) Engineer's Day
    (b) Teacher's Day
    (c) Science Day
    (d) Air Force Day

20. Who among the following is known as The Enlightened One?
    (a) Lord Buddha
    (b) Mahatma Gandhi
    (c) Mahavir
    (d) Jawaharlal Nehru

21. Which was the first country to make a Constitution?
    (a) India
    (b) United States of America
    (c) United Kingdom
    (d) France

22. Which one of the following is the second smallest continent of the world in terms of area?
    (a) Asia   (b) Europe
    (c) Africa   (d) Antarctica

23. The term 'Penalty stroke' is used in which of the following sports?
    (a) Baseball   (b) Hockey
    (c) Cricket   (d) Chess

24. .... is the second largest state of India by area.
    (a) Uttar Pradesh
    (b) Madhya Pradesh
    (c) Rajasthan
    (d) Maharashtra

25. Dipa Karmakar is associated with which of the following sports?
    (a) Steeplechase   (b) Squash
    (c) Gymnastics   (d) Javelin Throw

26. Which among the following is the smallest ocean of the world?
    (a) Pacific   (b) Indian
    (c) Atlantic   (d) Arctic

27. Which of the following sikh Gurus is considered as founder of Sikhism?
    (a) Guru Govind Singh
    (b) Guru Tegh Bahadur
    (c) Guru Nanak Dev
    (d) Guru Arjan Dev

28. Wright Brothers invented ....
    (a) Gun   (b) Battle Tank
    (c) Ships   (d) Airplane

29. Which gas is used in Air balloons?.
    (a) Helium   (b) Oxygen
    (c) Nitrogen   (d) Argon

30. The food pipe transports food from the mouth to the stomach. What is the other name for the food pipe?
    (a) Duodenum
    (c) Appendix
    (c) Oesophagus
    (d) Pancreas

31. A piece of stone and/or iron travelling through space that moves through the Earth's atmosphere is ....
    (a) Planet   (b) Sun
    (c) Moon   (d) Meteor

32. Which of the following books is written by great author William Shakespeare?
    (a) Julius Caesar
    (b) Invisible Man
    (c) Wings of Fire
    (d) None of the above

33. Who built Konark Sun Temple?
    (a) Narasimhadeva Varman
    (b) Rajendra Chola
    (c) Ashoka
    (d) Krishnadevaraya

34. Which one of the following is the main cause of Acid Rain?
    (a) Noise pollution
    (b) Water pollution
    (c) Land pollution
    (d) Air pollution

35. .... is an imaginery line divides the Earth into two equal parts?
    (a) Tropic of Cancer
    (b) Equator
    (c) Tropic of Capricon
    (d) All of the above

36. Which among the following is not a fossil fuel?
    (a) Coal   (b) Petroleum
    (c) Natural Gas   (d) Uranium

37. What should be the minimum age of the candidate to be elected as Chief Minister of any state?
    (a) 21 years   (b) 30 years
    (c) 28 years   (d) 25 years

38. Which is highest gallantry award for the personnel of armed forces in India?
    (a) Ashoka Chakra
    (b) Maha Vir Chakra
    (c) Param Vir Chakra
    (d) Kirti Chakra

39. Name the first super computer developed in India.
    (a) Eka   (b) Param
    (c) Aaditya   (d) Pratyush

40. Abhinav Bindra won India's first individual Olympic Gold Medal in ....
    (a) Archery   (b) Shooting
    (c) Wrestling   (d) Boxing

41. Match List I with List II.

List I		List II
A. System Software	1.	Pen Drive
B. Application	2.	Windows 7
C. Storage Device	3.	Microsoft Office

Codes

	A	B	C			A	B	C
(a)	2	3	1		(b)	3	1	2
(c)	2	1	3		(d)	1	2	3

42. Consider the following statements.

1. Sun is the good source of Vitamin D.

2. Milk is a good source of calcium for human body.

Which of the following statements is/are correct?
(a) Only 1　　　(b) Only 2
(c) Both 1 and 2　　(d) Neither 1 nor 2

43. Which of the given statement is true?

1. We cannot hear any sound on Moon as it does not have an atmosphere.

2. We can only see one side of the Moon from the Earth.

Codes
(a) Only 1　　　(b) Only 2
(c) Both 1 and 2　　(d) None of these

44. Select the correct statement from the given statements.

Statement 1 Geeta Phogat is a very famous boxer.

Statement 2 Geeta Phogat is from Haryana.
(a) 1 is correct　　(b) 2 is correct
(c) Both 1 and 2 are incorrect
(d) 1 is incorrect but 2 is correct

45. Which of the following pair is matched correctly?

1. Keyboard – Input Device

2. Web Camera – Output Device

3. DVD – Storage Device

Codes
(a) Only 1 and 2　　(b) Only 2 and 3
(c) Only 1 and 3　　(d) All of these

46. Select the correct statement from the given statements.

Statement 1 Carbon dioxide creates greenhouse effect in the atmosphere.

Statement 2 Carbon dioxide gas is present in bulk amount in the atmosphere.
(a) 1 is correct
(b) 2 is correct
(c) 1 is correct and 2 is incorrect
(d) Both 1 and 2 are correct

47. Match List I with List II.

List I (Events related to Buddha)		List II (Place)
A. Birth of Buddha	1.	Bodh Gaya
B. Enlightenment	2.	Lumbini
C. First Sermon	3.	Kushinagar (or Kasla)
D. Death of Buddha	4.	Sarnath

Codes

	A	B	C	D
(a)	2	1	3	4
(b)	1	3	4	2
(c)	2	1	4	3
(d)	4	2	1	3

48. Match List I with List II.

List I (Rulers)		List II (Dynasty)
A.	Prithviraj	1. Slave
B.	Jahangir	2. Gupta
C.	Skandagupt	3. Mughal
D.	Qutub-ud-din Aibak	4. Chauhan

Codes

	A	B	C	D
(a)	3	4	1	2
(b)	2	3	4	1
(c)	4	3	2	1
(d)	1	2	3	4

49. Consider the following statements.

1. There are only 5 rings present in the Olympic flag.

2. The first Olympic games were held in Athens,Greece.

Which of the following statements is/are correct?

(a) Only 1   (b) Only 2
(c) Both 1 and 2   (d) Neither 1 nor 2

50. Match List I with List II.

List I (State)		List II (Capital)
A.	China	1.	Kathmandu
B.	Nepal	2.	Islamabad
C.	Pakistan	3.	New Delhi
D.	India	4.	Beijing

Codes

	A	B	C	D			A	B	C	D
(a)	4	3	2	1		(b)	3	2	4	1
(c)	2	3	1	4		(d)	4	1	2	3

PRACTICE SET 

1. The famous player Sakshi Malik is associated with which of the following sports?
   (a) Hockey (b) Chess
   (c) Wrestling (d) Pistol Event

2. Who was the first Indian to receive a Nobel Prize?
   (a) Mother Teresa
   (b) Hargobind Tagore
   (c) CV Raman
   (d) Rabindranath Tagore

3. Which among the following is NOT the name of layer of Earth?
   (a) Mountain (b) Crust
   (c) Mantle (d) Core

4. Which one of the following is NOT a type of hardware?
   (a) Monitor (b) Keyboard
   (c) Google Chrome (d) UPS

5. The Panchayati Raj System in India is an institution of ………. .
   (a) Union Government
   (b) State Government
   (c) Central Government
   (d) Local Government

6. Igneous, Sedimentary and Metamorphic all are example of ……… .
   (a) Climate (b) Rocks
   (c) Temperature (d) Pollution

7. Titan is one of the moons of ……… .
   (a) Jupiter (b) Saturn
   (c) Venus (d) Earth

8. Who among the following is the writer of the book Hind Swaraj?
   (a) Jawaharlal Nehru
   (b) Mahatma Gandhi
   (c) Rabindranath Tagore
   (d) Subhash Chandra Bose

9. If there is no Sun in the sky, the colour of the sky would be ……… .
   (a) blue (b) orange (c) black (d) green

10. Which type of lens are used in myopia or Nearsightedness eye condition?
    (a) Concave (b) Convex
    (c) Plano Concave (d) None of these

11. The Caves of Ajanta and Ellora are located in ……… .
    (a) Nasik (b) Mumbai
    (c) Aurangabad (d) Pune

12. WWE stands for ……… .
    (a) World Wrestling Enterprises
    (b) World Wide Enterprises
    (c) World Wrestling Entertainment
    (d) None of the above

13. Which one of the following is the second biggest river of the world?
    (a) Mississippi River (b) Yangtze River
    (c) Danube River (d) Amazon River

14. How many Tirthankars are their in Jainism?
    (a) Thirty   (b) Twenty–four
    (c) Ten   (d) Twelve

15. 'National Education Day' is celebrated on ....
    (a) 12th November
    (b) 11th November
    (c) 5th November
    (d) 29th November

16. Which one of the following was the last Mughal Emperor?
    (a) Babur
    (b) Humayun
    (c) Aurenjeb
    (d) Bahadur Shah II

17. The Sambhar lake is located in which of the following states?
    (a) Rajasthan   (b) Gujarat
    (c) Uttar Pradesh   (d) Sikkim

18. Kathak is a classical dance form which originated in the Indian state of ....
    (a) Himachal Pradesh
    (b) Maharashtra
    (c) Madhya Pradesh
    (d) Uttar Pradesh

19. On which date 'National Science Day' is celebrated?
    (a) 5th May   (b) 15 th March
    (c) 5th January   (d) 28th February

20. Which of the following is a Non-renewable Resource?
    (a) Nuclear Power   (b) Hydropower
    (c) Natural Gas   (d) Tidal Energy

21. Who was the first woman to climb Mount Everest?
    (a) Arunima Sinha
    (b) Janet Yellen
    (c) Junko Tabei
    (d) Margaret Thatcher

22. Which one of the following ocean water is mostly found in frozen state?
    (a) Indian Ocean   (b) Pacific Ocean
    (c) Arctic Ocean   (d) Atlantic Ocean

23. Largest Port in India is located in ....
    (a) Mumbai   (b) Chennai
    (c) Kandla   (d) Kolkata

24. How many Gurus are there in Sikh Religion?
    (a) 9   (b) 5
    (c) 10   (d) 13

25. .... was the freedom fighter who started the revolt in the year 1857?
    (a) Mangal Pandey   (b) Bhagat Singh
    (c) Lala Lajpat Rai (d) Sardar Patel

26. The Olympic games held after every how many years?
    (a) 2 years   (b) 3 years
    (c) 4 years   (d) 5 years

27. Which is the largest lake in the world?
    (a) Victoria lake
    (b) Caspian sea
    (c) Baikal lake
    (d) Superior lake

28. The Gol Gumbad (Gumbaz) is located at ....
    (a) Allahabad   (b) Agra
    (c) Bijapur   (d) Delhi

29. A mixture of two or more metals is called an ………． .
    (a) alloy
    (b) mixture
    (c) solution
    (d) All of the above

30. Which system includes the brain and spinal cord?
    (a) Nervous system
    (b) Respitory system
    (c) Muscular system
    (d) Digestive system

31. Which of the following is the part of our Solar System?
    (a) Sun   (b) Comets
    (c) Asteroids   (d) All of these

32. Which among the following is the author of the famous book 'Cindrella'?
    (a) Ruskin Bond
    (b) Rudyard Kipling
    (c) Wilhelm Grimm
    (d) J K Rowling

33. What is the minimum age required for the candidate to be a Vice President of India?
    (a) 35 years   (b) 30 years
    (c) 25 years   (d) 50 years

34. The process of gradual increase in the Earth's temperature is called………． .
    (a) Pollution
    (b) Green house effect
    (c) Global warming
    (d) Acid rain

35. Which one of the following software programs attempt to identify, detect and prevent attacks on our computer?
    (a) Virus
    (b) Spam
    (c) Spyware
    (d) Antivirus

36. Which of the following is not a green house gas?
    (a) Carbon dioxide   (b) Methane
    (c) Nitrous Oxide
    (d) Carbon Monoxide

37. The Pulitzer Prize is associated with which of the following field?
    (a) Environmental protection
    (b) Olympic Games
    (c) Journalism
    (d) Civil Aviation

38. Which one of the following is NOT an example of Software?
    (a) Modem
    (b) Spreadsheets
    (c) Antivirus
    (d) Language Translator

39. Mississippi river is the longest river of
    (a) Asia   (b) Africa
    (c) North America   (d) Europe

40. Back flip : Gymnastic :: ………． : Swimming.
    (a) Flag kick
    (b) Knock out
    (c) Ace
    (d) Back stroke

41. Select the correct statement from the given statements.

Statement 1 The Governor of a state in India has the power to appoint judges of High court.

Statement 2 The Governor of a state in India is appointed by President.

Codes
(a) Only 1   (b) Only 2
(c) Both 1 and 2   (d) Neither 1 nor 2

42. Match the following.

	Country		Capital
A.	Sweden	1.	Stockholm
B.	France	2.	Ottawa
C.	Canada	3.	Paris

Codes
	A	B	C			A	B	C
(a)	1	3	2		(b)	3	1	2
(c)	2	1	3		(d)	1	2	3

43. Which of the following statement is correct?

Statement 1 World's first electronic computer was ENIAC.

Statement 2 The first generation of computers were very large in size.

Codes
(a) Only 1   (b) Only 2
(c) Both 1 and 2   (d) None of these

44. Select the incorrect match among the following options.
(a) Keyboard   –   Input device
(b) Printer   –   Output device
(c) Mouse   –   Processing device
(d) None of the above

45. Select the correct statement from the given statements.

Statement 1 Qutubuddin Aibak is first king of Slave dynasty in Delhi.

Statement 2 Raziya Sultan was only daughter of Qutubuddin Aibak.

Codes
(a) Only 1
(b) Only 2
(c) Both 1 and 2
(d) Neither 1 nor 2

46. Match the following.

	List I		List II
A.	Dal Lake	1.	Ladakh
B.	Pangong Lake	2.	Maharashtra
C.	Lonar Lake	3.	Kashmir

Codes
	A	B	C
(a)	2	3	1
(b)	3	1	2
(c)	1	3	2
(d)	3	2	1

47. Consider the following statements.
1. Rotation of Earth causes change in day and night.
2. Rotation of Earth causes rise and fall of tides everyday.

Which of the statements given above is/are correct?
(a) Only 1
(b) Only 2
(c) Both 1 and 2
(d) Neither 1 nor 2

48. Consider the following statements.

1. There are three levels of government is present in India.

2. The Supreme Court is the apex court in India.

Which of the statements given above is/are correct?

(a) Only 1   (b) Only 2
(c) Both 1 and 2   (d) Neither 1 nor 2

49. Match List I with List II.

List I (Term)		**List II** (Sport)	
A.	Free Kick	1.	Chess
B.	Dunk	2.	Shooting
C.	Bull's eye	3.	Basketball
D.	Pawns	4.	Football

Codes

	A	B	C	D
(a)	4	3	2	1
(b)	2	3	4	1
(c)	3	4	1	2
(d)	1	2	3	4

50. Which of the following statement is correct?

1. Iron gets rusting because of presence of water vapour in air.

2. The metal Brass is an alloy of zinc and copper.

Codes

(a) Only 1
(b) Only 2
(c) Both 1 and 2
(d) None of the above

Answers

Chapter 1   Famous Rulers and Freedom Fighters

1. (c)	2. (a)	3. (c)	4. (a)	5. (b)	6. (c)	7. (c)	8. (a)	9. (b)	10. (c)
11. (a)	12. (a)	13. (a)	14. (a)	15. (c)	16. (a)	17. (b)	18. (d)	19. (b)	20. (b)
21. (a)	22. (a)	23. (b)	24. (c)	25. (c)	26. (c)	27. (b)	28. (b)		

Chapter 2   Religion and Culture

1. (a)	2. (c)	3. (c)	4. (b)	5. (c)	6. (a)	7. (d)	8. (b)	9. (a)	10. (a)
11. (c)	12. (c)	13. (b)	14. (a)	15. (a)	16. (c)	17. (b)	18. (a)	19. (b)	20. (a)
21. (b)	22. (b)	23. (a)	24. (d)	25. (a)	26. (b)	27. (b)	28. (b)	29. (c)	30. (a)

Chapter 3   Buildings and Monuments

1. (b)	2. (a)	3. (b)	4. (a)	5. (a)	6. (d)	7. (a)	8. (b)	9. (a)	10. (a)
11. (c)	12. (a)	13. (b)	14. (b)	15. (d)	16. (b)	17. (a)	18. (b)	19. (c)	20. (b)
21. (a)	22. (a)	23. (b)	24. (a)	25. (a)	26. (c)	27. (a)	28. (a)	29. (a)	30. (a)
31. (d)									

Chapter 4   Solar System

1. (b)	2. (c)	3. (d)	4. (b)	5. (a)	6. (c)	7. (b)	8. (b)	9. (a)	10. (b)
11. (c)	12. (a)	13. (c)	14. (c)	15. (d)	16. (a)	17. (b)	18. (b)	19. (a)	20. (a)
21. (c)	22. (b)	23. (a)	24. (a)	25. (b)	26. (c)	27. (c)	28. (a)	29. (a)	

Chapter 5   Earth and its Movement

1. (b)	2. (c)	3. (b)	4. (b)	5. (b)	6. (b)	7. (a)	8. (b)	9. (b)	10. (a)
11. (c)	12. (c)	13. (a)	14. (a)	15. (c)	16. (c)	17. (b)	18. (b)	19. (c)	20. (a)
21. (d)	22. (b)	23. (b)	24. (a)						

Chapter 6   Continents and Oceans

1. (c)	2. (b)	3. (b)	4. (a)	5. (b)	6. (b)	7. (d)	8. (a)	9. (b)	10. (d)
11. (c)	12. (d)	13. (c)	14. (d)	15. (b)	16. (c)	17. (b)	18. (d)	19. (a)	20. (c)
21. (d)	22. (c)	23. (d)	24. (c)						

Chapter 7   Rivers and Lakes

1. (c)	2. (c)	3. (c)	4. (a)	5. (d)	6. (b)	7. (b)	8. (c)	9. (c)	10. (d)
11. (c)	12. (b)	13. (c)	14. (a)	15. (a)	16. (d)	17. (c)	18. (b)	19. (b)	20. (c)
21. (d)	22. (d)	23. (b)	24. (c)	25. (a)					

Chapter 8   Our Environment

1. (b)	2. (a)	3. (a)	4. (b)	5. (c)	6. (a)	7. (c)	8. (a)	9. (c)	10. (c)
11. (b)	12. (b)	13. (d)	14. (d)	15. (b)	16. (c)	17. (d)	18. (d)	19. (a)	20. (b)
21. (a)	22. (a)	23. (a)	24. (c)	25. (c)					

Chapter 9   Our Government

1. (b)	2. (c)	3. (a)	4. (b)	5. (a)	6. (c)	7. (c)	8. (b)	9. (c)	10. (b)
11. (b)	12. (c)	13. (b)	14. (a)	15. (b)	16. (a)	17. (c)	18. (c)	19. (c)	20. (d)

Chapter 10   General Science

1. (b)	2. (b)	3. (c)	4. (a)	5. (d)	6. (b)	7. (c)	8. (b)	9. (a)	10. (a)
11. (c)	12. (b)	13. (c)	14. (a)	15. (b)	16. (c)	17. (c)	18. (a)	19. (c)	20. (d)
21. (a)	22. (d)	23. (b)	24. (a)	25. (a)	26. (b)	27. (a)	28. (a)	29. (a)	30. (b)
31. (d)	32. (a)	33. (b)	34. (b)	35. (b)	36. (b)	37. (d)	38. (c)	39. (b)	40. (d)
41. (b)	42. (c)	43. (b)	44. (b)	45. (d)	46. (b)	47. (a)	48. (b)	49. (a)	

Chapter 11   Computers

1. (a)	2. (c)	3. (a)	4. (c)	5. (b)	6. (a)	7. (a)	8. (c)	9. (c)	10. (c)
11. (a)	12. (a)	13. (b)	14. (c)	15. (d)	16. (b)	17. (c)	18. (c)	19. (c)	20. (b)
21. (d)	22. (d)	23. (b)	24. (b)	25. (b)	26. (d)	27. (c)	28. (d)		

Chapter 12   General Knowledge

1. (c)	2. (b)	3. (b)	4. (b)	5. (a)	6. (b)	7. (d)	8. (d)	9. (b)	10. (b)
11. (b)	12. (c)	13. (b)	14. (b)	15. (d)	16. (c)	17. (c)	18. (b)	19. (b)	20. (c)
21. (c)	22. (b)	23. (c)	24. (a)	25. (d)	26. (c)	27. (c)	28. (d)	29. (c)	30. (c)
31. (c)	32. (b)	33. (d)	34. (c)	35. (c)	36. (d)	37. (b)	38. (d)	39. (c)	40. (d)
41. (c)	42. (a)	43. (c)	44. (a)	45. (b)	46. (c)	47. (c)	48. (c)	49. (c)	50. (b)
51. (c)	52. (b)	53. (c)	54. (c)	55. (a)	56. (a)	57. (b)			

Chapter 13   Books and Authors

1. (c)	2. (b)	3. (a)	4. (b)	5. (b)	6. (c)	7. (b)	8. (d)	9. (b)	10. (a)
11. (c)	12. (c)	13. (b)	14. (b)	15. (a)					

Chapter 14   Important Days and Dates

1. (b)	2. (d)	3. (b)	4. (c)	5. (a)	6. (c)	7. (a)	8. (d)	9. (b)	10. (c)
11. (c)	12. (c)	13. (a)	14. (b)	15. (c)	16. (b)	17. (b)	18. (c)	19. (c)	20. (d)

Chapter 15   Awards and Honours

1. (d)	2. (a)	3. (d)	4. (b)	5. (a)	6. (c)	7. (d)	8. (b)	9. (b)	10. (c)
11. (a)	12. (b)	13. (a)	14. (a)	15. (a)	16. (a)	17. (d)			

Chapter 16   Sports

1. (b)	2. (a)	3. (b)	4. (c)	5. (a)	6. (c)	7. (a)	8. (a)	9. (a)	10. (a)
11. (b)	12. (a)	13. (b)	14. (a)	15. (b)	16. (c)	17. (b)	18. (a)	19. (b)	20. (a)
21. (b)	22. (a)	23. (c)	24. (c)	25. (b)					

Practice Set 1

1. (d)	2. (b)	3. (d)	4. (c)	5. (a)	6. (d)	7. (c)	8. (d)	9. (d)	10. (d)
11. (d)	12. (b)	13. (b)	14. (a)	15. (b)	16. (c)	17. (c)	18. (b)	19. (c)	20. (a)
21. (b)	22. (b)	23. (b)	24. (b)	25. (c)	26. (d)	27. (c)	28. (d)	29. (a)	30. (c)
31. (d)	32. (a)	33. (a)	34. (d)	35. (b)	36. (d)	37. (d)	38. (c)	39. (b)	40. (b)
41. (a)	42. (c)	43. (c)	44. (d)	45. (c)	46. (c)	47. (c)	48. (c)	49. (c)	50. (d)

Practice Set 2

1. (c)	2. (d)	3. (a)	4. (c)	5. (d)	6. (b)	7. (b)	8. (b)	9. (c)	10. (a)
11. (c)	12. (c)	13. (d)	14. (b)	15. (b)	16. (d)	17. (a)	18. (d)	19. (d)	20. (c)
21. (c)	22. (c)	23. (a)	24. (c)	25. (a)	26. (c)	27. (b)	28. (c)	29. (a)	30. (a)
31. (d)	32. (c)	33. (a)	34. (c)	35. (d)	36. (d)	37. (c)	38. (a)	39. (c)	40. (d)
41. (c)	42. (a)	43. (c)	44. (c)	45. (d)	46. (b)	47. (c)	48. (c)	49. (a)	50. (c)

9 789325 519442